Retaining Your Best College Professors

Retaining Your Best College Professors

You Worked Hard to Recruit Them; Now How Do You Keep Them?

Jeffrey L. Buller

ROWMAN & LITTLEFIELD
Lanham • Boulder • New York • London

Published by Rowman & Littlefield
An imprint of The Rowman & Littlefield Publishing Group, Inc.
4501 Forbes Boulevard, Suite 200, Lanham, Maryland 20706
www.rowman.com

6 Tinworth Street, London, SE11 5AL, United Kingdom

Copyright © 2021 by Jeffrey L. Buller

All rights reserved. No part of this book may be reproduced in any form or by any electronic or mechanical means, including information storage and retrieval systems, without written permission from the publisher, except by a reviewer who may quote passages in a review.

British Library Cataloguing in Publication Information Available

Library of Congress Cataloging-in-Publication Data

Names: Buller, Jeffrey L., author.
Title: Retaining your best college professors : you worked hard to recruit them; now how do you keep them? / Jeffrey L. Buller.
Description: Lanham, Maryland : Rowman & Littlefield, 2021. | Includes bibliographical references and index. | Summary: "This book addresses why higher education currently has a faculty retention problem and then explores the strategies needed to address that problem"—Provided by publisher.
Identifiers: LCCN 2021024312 (print) | LCCN 2021024313 (ebook) | ISBN 9781475862003 (cloth) | ISBN 9781475862010 (paperback) | ISBN 9781475862027 (epub)
Subjects: LCSH: College teacher turnover—United States—Prevention. | College teachers—Job satisfaction—United States.
Classification: LCC LB2335.3 .B85 2021 (print) | LCC LB2335.3 (ebook) | DDC 378.1/20973—dc23
LC record available at https://lccn.loc.gov/2021024312
LC ebook record available at https://lccn.loc.gov/2021024313

For Kenneth R. Bartlett, who taught me everything I know about faculty engagement (and a good deal more)

Contents

Preface	ix
Introduction	xi
Chapter 1: The Faculty Retention Problem	1
Chapter 2: Retaining a Diverse Faculty	11
Chapter 3: Best Practices in Onboarding and Orientation	25
Chapter 4: Providing Support at Critical Points	37
Chapter 5: Promoting Faculty Engagement	65
Chapter 6: Part-Time Faculty, Adjuncts, and Full-Time Temps	79
Chapter 7: Creating a Culture of Hiring and Retaining the Best	93
Index	105
About the Author	113
Other Books by Jeffrey L. Buller	115
More about ATLAS	109

Preface

Personnel costs are by far the largest component of the higher education budget. In the typical department or college, salaries and benefits constitute at least 80 percent of the budget and may even reach 90 or 95 percent. That's why enormous expense is devoted to making sure that the faculty members who are hired are the best available. Searches are expensive and require time that those conducting them could otherwise spend on their teaching and research.

That's also why it's so frustrating to academic leaders when they've made every effort and invested both time and money to hire exactly the right person for the job only to have that person leave for another position in a few years. As one participant in a workshop I was conducting on faculty searches told me once the session was over, "Sure, I can do all of this to recruit the right faculty members. But once I hire them, how do I keep them?"

This book is an attempt to answer that question. It's the result of thirty-eight years of professional experience, research into proven best practices developed by colleges and universities of all kinds, and lessons learned from administrators who have discovered at great cost what doesn't work.

What the reader will learn in the pages that follow is that there are practical steps he or she can take to decrease faculty attrition while increasing faculty engagement. Some of these steps require major systemic changes but many don't. Some of these steps require significant investment but many don't. What I hope *Retaining Your Best College Professors* will do is serve as a kind of tool kit from which faculty members and administrators will pick and choose the strategies that will work best for them and their unique situations. They will encounter dozens of suggestions and discover enough good ideas to make a real difference in their faculty retention rates.

Some of the best college professors you can find are probably already on your payroll, and it costs far less to *keep* a good faculty member than to *recruit and hire* a new one. As budgets become tighter and competition for talent becomes greater, all of us who work in higher education have an obligation to use our resources most effectively by retaining the highly marketable college professors who are already working at our schools.

Introduction

Administrators who are worried about faculty retention don't want theories and jargon; they want answers. They want to know what works so that they can adopt it and what doesn't work so that they can avoid it. *Retaining Your Best College Professors* has been written in such a way as to provide clear answers to the question "What should I do next?" and guide readers in developing their own strategies for improving faculty retention.

This book begins with a survey of the faculty retention problem that is plaguing colleges and universities of all kinds. It points out that, while schools devote significant resources to promote *student* retention, the amount of time and effort devoted to *faculty* retention often pales in comparison. And yet, unnecessary faculty searches require substantial expenditures both in terms of one-time costs (for posting position announcements, hosting finalists, and taking search committee members away from other tasks they could be performing for the institution) and ongoing costs (since replacement faculty members typically receive higher salaries than the person they're replacing). If academic leaders want to get serious about controlling their costs, controlling faculty attrition is a good place to start.

The book then examines several major obstacles to faculty retention and suggests ways of avoiding them. Mistakes are often made with regard to the support given to minority faculty members, the procedures used to onboard all new faculty members to the institution, and the efforts made (or, more frequently, *not* made) to increase faculty engagement. Attention is also paid to the distinctive challenges encountered in retaining contingent faculty members (i.e., temporary employees regardless of whether they work part-time or full-time). Finally, suggestions are provided for what academic leaders should be doing *right now* even while they work on developing sustainable, long-term approaches to faculty retention.

Retaining Your Best College Professors is intended for anyone working in higher education: faculty members who want to retain their colleagues, administrators who want to decrease the amount of money they're devoting to repeated faculty searches, and members of governing boards who want to change institution policies in a way that best suits the organizational culture in higher education. The book can be used by:

- Individuals either for their own professional development or in leadership development programs
- Students of higher education leadership as a textbook in decision-making and problem-solving
- Human resources personnel who wish to discover why retention strategies that often work with the staff don't always work as well with the faculty

The author would like to thank his editor at Rowman & Littlefield, Tom Koerner, for his enthusiastic support throughout now more than ten books; Sandra McClain for her countless hours of editorial and research assistance; and the many academic leaders who have attended the author's workshops and webinars over the years, providing many helpful suggestions and insights.

Chapter 1

The Faculty Retention Problem

It's a problem we've all experienced. You invested a great deal of time and effort in conducting an exhaustive search for the best professor you could find, hired an excellent candidate, and then had to go through that entire process again a few years later when the faculty member left to take a job somewhere else.

Many colleges and universities devote substantial resources to retaining students, but fewer of them are as proactive when it comes to retaining faculty. And yet, faculty attrition can be just as costly to an institution as student attrition. The process of searching for and hiring new professors is expensive and time consuming. In the vast majority of cases, the new faculty member will require a salary higher than the person he or she is replacing. And start-up costs, particularly in the natural sciences, can require a tremendous investment every time a new faculty member is hired.

But it isn't just a matter of money that makes the problem of faculty retention so severe. When good professors leave a college or university they take their knowledge of institutional history with them. They often take their reputation for important research with them. And, in too many cases, they take a bitter experience with them that can damage a school's reputation with prospective students, donors, and faculty members.

At public colleges and universities, statewide budget cuts and the abolition of tenure rights can result in a wholesale defection of a school's most prestigious faculty. For example, in the first quarter of the twenty-first century, the University of Wisconsin–Madison (UW) found itself affected by a "perfect storm" of budget cuts, legislative attacks on tenure, and national reductions in funding for major grants programs.

> The majority of [budget] cuts were focused on the educational side, causing a decrease in staff, faculty and advisors and an increase in class sizes, [the university's chancellor, Rebecca] Blank said.

"At a time when almost all the other states around us are increasing their higher education funding and investing, every year that we are filling budget holes rather than investing in new ideas and new issues and new opportunities for students, we are falling behind our competitors and that is a problem," Blank said. . . .

UW recently lost its National Science Foundation ranking as one of the top five research universities, a stumble that Blank links with Wisconsin's political climate and a loss of faculty.

Nearly 10 percent of UW faculty received outside offers last year, which Blank said is a result of budget cuts and the national media storm after changes in state tenure policy.

She said when the state "tore up" tenure rules and gave Regents the responsibility of rewriting them, many faculty members were upset and the media misled people to believe tenure was completely eliminated. . . .

UW's top faculty bring in millions of dollars in research funding, so the loss of certain members can have a significant impact on the ability of the university to compete in the research field. She said UW lost a few of its top grant receivers and these departures contributed to UW's falling ranking. (Duffey and Neinfeldt, 2016)

The average *annual* faculty turnover rates at schools in the University of Wisconsin System ranged from 5 percent to 9 percent, with the UW Extension program suffering a dramatic 24 percent attrition rate in *2018 alone* (Meyerhofer, 2018).

Similar challenges affected the University of North Carolina (UNC) System, where a study found that the following factors were driving increased attrition rates among faculty members:

- Frustration was expressed with poor pay raises and issues of salary compression.
- Retirement benefits were found to be adequate but not health insurance benefits.
- There was limited support expressed for professional development and sabbaticals. . . .
- Tenure guidelines and expectations were reported to be unclear, and faculty felt the need for support and more follow-up on their progress, and felt tenure expectations were a "moving target."
- The majority of faculty were dissatisfied with efforts to enhance diversity by their institutions and perceived major weaknesses in several areas. (Trotman and Brown, 2005)

In the decade and a half following that study, other factors exacerbated the problem of faculty retention throughout the North Carolina System. An academic fraud scandal involving the University of North Carolina at Chapel Hill's football team and courses offered by the Department of African and Afro-American Studies caused the institution to be placed on probation by its accrediting agency, the Southern Association of Colleges and Schools Commission on Colleges.

A controversy over the fate of a UNC statue honoring students who fought for the confederacy led to conflict between the faculty and the governing board, with a group of faculty and students having the board's proposed solution overturned in court. The struggle between faculty members and what they viewed as an overly activist board of governors—coupled with reduced research funding at the federal level and modest salary increases at the university—led a number of high-profile professors and administrators to either step down from their positions or leave the institution entirely.

> [Leslie] Parise's decision to step down [as chair of the faculty] comes amidst turnover for the UNC–Chapel Hill campus administration and UNC System leadership. Margaret Spellings was replaced as system president by William Roper—former dean of the UNC School of Medicine—earlier this year. Former UNC–Chapel Hill chancellor Carol Folt announced in mid-January she would be resigning at the end of the semester. The UNC System Board of Governors accelerated that timeline to the end of January after Folt ordered the removal of the remaining base of the Confederate monument known as Silent Sam from the Chapel Hill campus. Folt has since been named the next president of the University of Southern California. (Hodge, 2019)

In certain disciplines, the problem of faculty attrition is even worse. A study conducted in 2017 by the Alliance for Academic Internal Medicine found that "average attrition ranges from 25% to 30% at medical schools and teaching hospitals as current faculty seriously consider leaving the academic environment" (Brod, Lemeshow, and Binkley, 2017). Moreover, many programs suffer from their ability to retain highly qualified women and minorities as institutions compete to expand the diversity of their faculties.

Retention of minority faculty members is a significant challenge at many colleges and universities (Piercy, Giddings, Allen, Dixon, Meszaros, and Joest, 2005). The reasons cited for this attrition include a general lack of support, overt discrimination, incivility, and a climate that fails to support personal growth. But those are precisely the same factors that can lead to an increase in faculty attrition generally (O'Meara, Lounder, and Campbell, 2014).

A study conducted by Rensselaer Polytechnic Institute suggested that the median amount of time faculty members stay at a university is only eleven years, the first six or seven of which are typically consumed by the quest for tenure and promotion.

"This means if you hire 100 assistant professors tomorrow, in 11 years only 50 of them will still be at your school," said [Deborah] Kaminski, professor in the Department of Mechanical, Aerospace, and Nuclear Engineering . . . at Rensselaer. "This leakage rate is huge, and should be a big red flag to everyone in higher education. The problem is particularly acute for research universities, where recruitment is expensive and competitive start-up packages for new faculty members can be upward of $1 million." (Study in Journal *Science*, 2012)

High rates of faculty attrition aren't limited to American universities (see, for example, Singh and Mittal, 2017). What these results mean is that it's not uncommon for colleges and universities, regardless of their location, to lose roughly half of the faculty in little more than a decade. For many schools that rate of attrition entails an unsustainable amount of wasted resources, talent, and knowledge of institutional history. As academic leaders, we need to do better.

THE DROSS FACTOR

Compounding the struggle to retain good faculty members is another issue familiar to department chairs, deans, and provosts but rarely discussed, a problem that is sometimes referred to as the *Dross Factor*. The most accomplished faculty members are highly marketable. Schools will sometimes lure them away with large salaries and other benefits in order to bring increased prestige (or perhaps simply larger grants) to their institutions. But what about the faculty members who remain?

Many of the faculty members who aren't sufficiently marketable to attract highly competitive offers from other colleges and universities are quite good, even very good. They had to demonstrate their strengths in order to be hired, retained, and promoted. But they may not perform at quite the level of their colleagues who are actively recruited by other institutions. As a result, the percentage of tenured faculty members who are very good, but not extraordinary, can increase over time, particularly at second- or third-tier institutions.

There is also a smaller number of faculty members who perform well enough to earn tenure and be promoted to the rank of associate professor but then, for whatever reason, stagnate in terms of teaching, research, or both. They don't perform poorly enough to be dismissed, but they also don't perform well enough to become distinguished. They remain, as some administrators have termed them, *terminal associate professors.*

The Dross Factor occurs when highly competitive faculty members can't be retained, but "terminal associate professors" and good-but-not-outstanding faculty members remain. In fact, that trend can sometimes intensify. At a certain point, a faculty—either within a certain discipline or across the entire institution—may become perceived as ordinary or "insufficiently distinguished," making it even more difficult to hire and retain professors at the top of their field.

The "gold" thus never comes to a school in the first place or is soon enticed to leave, while the "dross" remains behind. Wealthy, highly prestigious institutions become even more prestigious. Less wealthy institutions become burdened with a perception that their faculties are second rate.

Many people outside of higher education tend to exaggerate the impact of the Dross Factor. They assume that tenure guarantees that professors have a job regardless of the quality of their work. The truth is that the vast majority of faculty members care deeply about their students and are highly dedicated to their work. It's simply not true that tenure and long-term contracts diminish the quality of higher education.

Nevertheless, academic leaders are right to be concerned about the mobility of their faculty "stars." No one wants to be in the position of heading a program where the best professors leave and the only people who stay are those with no options. So, the challenge becomes: How do we retain our most gifted faculty members even when other schools can pay them more or offer them better benefits?

SOME INITIAL ANSWERS

This question can't be answered by adopting a few quick fixes. As will be illustrated in the chapters that follow, other questions need to be asked first. What makes the faculty members you're hoping to retain so desirable? Are they members of minority groups? Do they bring other important attributes to your program? Where are they in their career paths: young superstars? mid-career professors with distinguished résumés? senior scholars who might be looking for new challenges? And is retaining a faculty member just in the best interests of your program or does it also help the faculty member herself?

In addition, some of the solutions to faculty retention are systemic and can't be implemented by the chair or dean alone. In Chapter 4, for example, the importance of creating new faculty ranks that go beyond the traditional divisions of assistant, associate, and full professor will be discussed. Implementing some of these changes and developing an institution-wide culture of faculty retention will take some time.

But if you don't *have* the luxury of time on your side—if you've got a highly prized faculty member who's on the verge of leaving *now*, for example—there are still some approaches you can take. You may not have enough budgetary discretion to match or exceed someone's salary expectations, but it's important to remember that that compensation isn't synonymous with income. There may be ways that you can reward your star faculty members that are more important to them than salary alone.

- *Reassigned time.* Many college professors feel that time is a more valuable commodity than money. A reduced course load, flexible work schedule, or research release may address the issues that have led the faculty member to consider leaving.
- *Reduced service obligation.* Of the three elements that compose the standard "academic triad"—teaching, research, and service—service often has the least satisfying time-to-rewards ratio. In other words, committee work can consume many hours throughout the week and yet matter relatively little when decisions are made about tenure, promotion, and merit increases. If you can free faculty members from most or all of their service obligations, they may find this type of compensation highly desirable.
- *Public recognition.* One theme that will be repeated throughout this book is that many faculty members leave an institution because they don't feel it appreciates them sufficiently. Counteract this impression by recognizing your star faculty members publicly. Discuss their contributions at meetings. Present them with certificates. Name a lecture series in their honor. Write an article about them for the alumni magazine. Recognitions cost you next to nothing, but they can be powerful in their impact.
- *Private recognition.* Other types of recognition are best done in private. Ask the president or provost to call the faculty member (or, even better, take the person to lunch) and sing his or her praises. Write a personalized note that describes the important contribution the faculty member has made to your program. Stop by the person's office and express your appreciation. You may think your faculty members already know how much you value their work, but it never hurts to tell them a few more times.
- *Solutions to work-life challenges.* Faculty members sometimes leave because their spouses can't find work or they need special care for their children or parents. Use your network to address these concerns. Open doors for the faculty member's spouse that lead to interviews or offers of employment. Contact social workers in your city or region to explore ways of meeting the faculty member's needs in caring for parents or children.
- *One-time investments.* Large salary increases are often difficult to make because they require a recurring investment. Every year the faculty member will continue to earn that higher salary, along with any other

increases that have been made in the meantime. But one-time investments can provide a lasting benefit without causing lasting strain on your budget. Purchase a piece of equipment that is important to the faculty member's teaching or research. Fund travel to a conference in some highly desirable location. Allow the faculty member to redecorate his or her office.

None of these suggestions will work in every case. But any of them can be used with any others. Imagine countering a faculty member's job offer with the opportunity to have a reduced teaching load and be released from all committee assignments for five years, a lecture series in his or her honor, a phone call from the president who tells the faculty member that he or she is invaluable, a handwritten letter of support from you, a new piece of equipment of the faculty member's choice, and funding to attend a conference in Paris.

Certainly your counter offer will entail substantial one-time costs. But will those costs be more than conducting a search for a replacement? Would the replacement cost the institution more by requiring a higher salary? And would a replacement be as good as your star faculty member? The investment you make today in helping to retain one of your highest performers is likely to continue paying dividends for many years to come.

OVERCOMING THE "LET 'EM LEAVE" PHILOSOPHY

Academic leaders will sometimes encounter colleagues who argue that it's actually counterproductive to take measures intended to stem faculty attrition. "If you give in to people's demands now," these colleagues say, "they will simply keep asking you for more in the future. Why would you want to keep anyone here who doesn't *want* to stay? It's better to let the person go and hire someone who's a better fit."

This perspective, which might be called the *"Let 'Em Leave" Philosophy*, isn't entirely misguided. Institutions can waste a substantial amount of resources giving in to the demands of faculty members who repeatedly use the threat of resignation to extort concessions such as higher salaries and reduced workload. Moreover, faculty members who've grudgingly agreed to stay only because of some increase in compensation aren't likely to demonstrate the kind of *intrinsic motivation* that will keep them highly engaged in the long run.

Nevertheless, applying the "Let 'Em Leave" Philosophy to *everyone* who's tempted by a position elsewhere can deprive a program of some of its most talented professors. Not every faculty member is alike. If academic leaders adopt precisely the same approach in each case of a faculty member considering other career options, they're not merely being consistent; they're also being inflexible and shortsighted.

The stars and superstars in our programs will be approached from time to time by other institutions who want to lure them away. It's only natural for someone with an impressive record of teaching, research, and service to wonder if "the grass may be greener" somewhere else. If you treat everyone who considers his or her options as a "traitor to the program," you're only going to encourage your best people to leave, not provide them with additional reasons to stay.

When a faculty member approaches you to tell you that he or she has an offer from another school—or when you're aware that someone is seriously exploring his or her career options—there are a number of questions you may want to ask yourself:

1. *How integral is this person to our program?* This question is a more objective way of asking, "How badly do I want this person to stay?" If you think only in terms of your own personal desires, your decision is more likely to be clouded by the type of relationship you have with the person, how you're feeling at that particular moment, and similar factors. If, on the other hand, you focus on the degree to which that person is integral to what your program has become, you increase the probability that you'll base your decision on rational, impartial considerations, not reasons that may be difficult to justify to others.
2. *What are the cost considerations involved?* As was noted earlier, conducting searches is expensive. It can be penny wise and pound foolish to reject a faculty member's reasonable request for a salary increase or other form of compensation if the alternative is to initiate a hiring process that will cost you even more in terms of time and resources. Weigh the trade-offs before making your decision.
3. *How often is the faculty member making this type of request?* Offering some type of concession to a phenomenal faculty member who's wondering about the wisdom of accepting another option is quite a different thing from continually being blackmailed by someone who uses external offers to demand repeated salary adjustments and other special favors. If a faculty member falls into the category of being good to very good but not exceptional, you may even want to say something like, "Okay. I'll see what I can do this one time. But we can't make adjustments like this repeatedly." But if the faculty member is truly one of your stars, then the first question above—How integral is this person to our program?—should take precedence.

CONCLUSION

Solving the problem of faculty attrition requires more than a quick fix. The suggestions outlined in this chapter offer a start, but they're *only* a start. In order to develop a system where faculty retention is a priority, academic leaders need to think differently about many of their most common assumptions concerning what faculty members want and need in order to succeed. In the chapters that follow, a comprehensive plan for retaining your best faculty members will be explained step-by-step.

Implementing that plan will require both time and institutional commitment. But it's ultimately in an institution's long-term interest, both financially and in terms of student success, for that commitment to become a priority.

KEY POINTS IN THIS CHAPTER

- The attrition rate for college professors is unacceptably high.
- Faculty members with strong records in teaching and research are highly marketable, and institutions often find it difficult to retain them.
- The expense of faculty searches, coupled with high start-up costs in many fields, makes a high rate of faculty retention unsustainable.
- Budget cuts, attacks on tenure rights, and activist governing boards have exacerbated this problem at many institutions.
- Second- and third-tier institutions often suffer worst from attrition of their best faculty members, leaving them with increasing percentages of faculty members who, although good, are not superstars.
- Short-term solutions to the faculty attrition problem include reassigned time, increased opportunities for faculty recognition, decreases in service obligations, one-time investments in equipment and travel, and solutions to work-life changes.
- Short-term solutions by themselves are not enough. Faculty retention requires an ongoing commitment by the institution and its leaders.

REFERENCES

Brod, H. C., Lemeshow, S., & Binkley, P. F. (2017). Determinants of faculty departure in an academic medical center: A time to event analysis. *The American Journal of Medicine. 130*(4), 488–493.

Duffey, M., & Neinfeldt, W. (2016). Blank links faculty retention issues, fall in research ranking to UW System budget cuts. *The Badger Herald.* https://bad

gerherald.com/features/2016/12/06/blank-links-cuts-to-uw-system-in-five-of-past-six-budgets-to-faculty-retention-issues-fall-from-high-research-ranking/.

Hodge, B. (2019). UNC faculty chair stepping down. *Chapelboro.com*. https://chapelboro.com/news/unc/unc-faculty-chair-stepping-down.

Meyerhofer, K. (2018). Which UW campuses saw the most faculty turnover in 2017–18 school year? *Wisconsin State Journal*. https://madison.com/wsj/news/local/education/university/which-uw-campuses-saw-the-most-faculty-turnover-in-/article_e136d0c4-d5e4-5373-9907-c2a92f59dd4c.html.

O'Meara, K., Lounder, A., & Campbell, C. M. (2014). To Heaven or Hell: Sensemaking about why faculty leave. *Journal of Higher Education. 85*(5), 603–632.

Piercy, F., Giddings, V., Allen, K., Dixon, B., Meszaros, P., & Joest, K. (2005). Improving campus climate to support faculty diversity and retention: A pilot program for new faculty. *Innovative Higher Education. 30*(1), 53–66.

Singh, R., & Mittal, R. K. (2017). Determinants of faculty retention: A study of engineering and management institutes in the state of Uttar Pradesh and NCR Delhi. *Techmind Research Society. 8*(2), 916–923.

Study in Journal *Science*: Rensselaer Polytechnic Institute. (2012). https://news.rpi.edu/luwakkey/2994.

Trotman, C.-A., & Brown, B. E. (2005). Faculty recruitment and retention: Concerns of early and mid-career faculty. *Research Dialogue*. https://pdfs.semanticscholar.org/f770/16b3615b1a3d3a0e483dc09454e594813788.pdf.

RESOURCES

Kaminski, D., & Geisler, C. (2012). Survival analysis of faculty retention in science and engineering by gender. *Science. 335*(6070), 864–866.

Pololi, L. H., Krupat, E., Civian, J. T., Ash A. S., & Brennan R. T. (2012). Why are a quarter of faculty considering leaving academic medicine? A study of their perceptions of institutional culture and intentions to leave at 26 representative U.S. medical schools. *Academic Medicine. 87*(7), 859–869.

Price, E. G., Gozu, A., Kern, D. E., Powe, N. R., Wand, G. S., Golden, S., & Cooper, L. A. (2005). The role of cultural diversity climate in recruitment, promotion, and retention of faculty in academic medicine. *Journal of General Internal Medicine. 20*(7), 565–571.

Soomro, T. R., & Ahmad, R. (2013). Faculty retention in higher education. *International Journal of Higher Education. 2*(2), 147–150.

Chapter 2

Retaining a Diverse Faculty

For more than thirty years, diversifying the faculty has been a major goal of most colleges and universities. Some institutions pursue diversity for all the right reasons: They want to provide their students with a multitude of perspectives, role models that students of all ethnicities can identify with, and opportunities that were too often denied to previous generations of scholars.

Other institutions want to diversify the faculty for more cynical reasons. They think that they might attract more students (and thus increase their tuition income) by having a faculty that appeals to a broader demographic. They seek designations like "minority-serving institution" or "Hispanic-serving institution" that can open the doors to additional grant opportunities and public-private partnerships. Or they diversify the faculty largely out of peer pressure. Since other colleges and universities have a less homogeneous professoriate, it can attract undesirable attention to be perceived as little better than an "old white boys' club."

Regardless of whether their reasons for seeking a more diverse faculty are admirable or cynical, many colleges and universities find that *recruiting* minority faculty members is only part of the challenge. *Retaining* minority faculty members can often be quite difficult since the pool of candidates is limited but the goal of achieving a highly qualified and diverse corps of instruction is highly competitive.

The fact is that too many institutions direct all their efforts and resources to the goal of hiring excellent members of minority groups but devote little if any energy to making sure that the faculty members they hire are satisfied once they receive their positions, have the resources they need, feel valued as members of the community, and receive the respect they deserve.

A LACK OF INFRASTRUCTURE

One reason why institutions sometimes fail to retain the minority faculty members they hire is that they don't have the type of infrastructure that makes it desirable for the faculty members to stay. They put all of their resources into *recruiting*, few of their resources into *retaining*.

To be sure, it's not only minority faculty members who need the right infrastructure in order to succeed. Everyone who is hired will need support in order to make that crucial transition from being a bright graduate student to a distinguished scholar. So, if retention of minority faculty members is a challenge at your institution, the first place to look when seeking a cause is whether the school is offering *all* of its new professors the following:

- **Onboarding** that's not condensed to a week or less but that continues for at least one full year. Good retention begins from the very moment a new faculty member arrives on campus. It's important to demonstrate that the institution's environment is welcoming and supportive (see Chapter 3).
- **Access to a mentor** who can help provide background on the school's culture and traditions, warn the new faculty member about political quagmires and other pitfalls that can complicate his or her career at the institution, open the right doors to the right people, and generally make the new hire feel welcome long after the excitement of the interview and contract offer has subsided.
- **Adjustment in responsibilities reflective of the institution's mission and aspirations.** Unless a new faculty member has already taught at another college or university, every course requires substantial new preparation. That ticking tenure clock means that the person's research agenda has to be pursued vigorously. And, due to the increased expectation that faculty members also help recruit students and raise external funds to support their programs, high service expectations begin almost immediately. The issue of workload alone sets up many new faculty members for failure. So, in light of what the institution is and wants to become, some adjustment in expectations seems reasonable. At a research-intensive institution, that adjustment might mean a reduced teaching load, not just for one semester or a single year, but every year until the faculty member's first promotion. At a "teaching first" institution, expectations for scholarly contributions should reflect the school's values. Too many colleges and universities *say* they value teaching most of all but require nearly as much research of their new hires as do large research universities. Expecting a faculty member to do it all doesn't

have to mean doing it *all at once*. The probationary pre-tenure should continue to be a time for the school to determine whether the faculty member has the potential of being a valued member of the community for the long term. But it should also be a time for the institution to allow the faculty member to grow into his or her new role as a college professor.

- **An appropriate level of research support**. Research-intensive universities receive large grants and produce significant numbers of peer-reviewed publications because they invest in research infrastructure. They have grant writers, budget officers, and training programs to help new faculty members learn how to tailor a proposal to the specific interests of each funding agency. Smaller institutions may not be able to provide such extensive support, but they can realize that graduate school doesn't always teach students everything they need to know about how to conduct research as a college professor. Writing a research paper for a class isn't exactly the same thing as writing an article for a journal. Writing a dissertation isn't exactly the same thing as writing a book. The better an institution can prepare its faculty members for making formal presentations at conferences, submitting proposals for grants and publications, and writing in the style expected by editors of major presses, the more likely it is that the institution will retain the faculty members it hires.
- **An appropriate level of social support.** Colleges and universities sometimes fall into the trap of thinking about college professors as mere providers of teaching, research, and service. But faculty members are three-dimensional human beings who are often rearing children, dealing with aging parents, and trying to build meaningful lives in their communities at the same time that they're developing their careers. Institutional approaches such as *tenure stop-clock policies* (i.e., allowing the faculty member to extend his or her tenure deadline for personal reasons) and free or reduced-cost childcare can, at least in theory, go a long way toward making faculty members want to stay at an institution. (See Chapter 4, however, for a discussion of why tenure stop-clock policies often backfire.) As of the publication date of this book, average annual costs of childcare in the United States ranged from about $10,000 to about $40,000 per year, depending on region. So, if a school is able to provide free childcare or to offer assistance with that cost, the result is equivalent to a far higher salary that might tempt the faculty member elsewhere. Tuition remission policies for dependents, spousal job placement services, and similar programs also reflect the institution's commitment to faculty members as people, not just as employees.

A LACK OF COMMUNITY

These attempts to provide the sort of infrastructure needed by all new faculty members are important for the retention of minority faculty members, but they're not enough. In order to understand why, engage in a short thought experiment. If you're not a member of a minority group, imagine for a moment that you are. And if you *are* a member of a minority group, imagine that—because of religion, country of origin, physical characteristics, accent, or some other quality—you're a member of a very small subset within your minority population.

Then reflect on the following:

- In this thought experiment, suppose that the vast majority of the people in your department, college or division, and institution have a very different view of the world from your own. People don't share your values and have different assumptions about what is important in life. In certain conversations, you find it challenging to relate to what other people are saying or to make them understand your own perspectives.
- Suppose that it is very difficult for you to find the types of food you like most, clothing that suits your taste and traditions, and even barbershops or hair salons that are familiar with the styles that suit you. Certainly, some of these needs can be met through online shopping, but consider the additional challenges posed when the Internet is your *only* option in many cases.
- Envision a scenario where your religion or life philosophy is extremely uncommon in your community. The nearest place of worship or fellowship for those sharing your belief system is more than a hundred miles away, and even those services or sessions are sparsely attended.
- You have few, if any, close friends at your institution because everywhere you go you feel like an outsider. Except for members of your immediate family, there is no one nearby with whom you can share these concerns.

The purpose of this thought experiment isn't to suggest that every member of a minority group at a college or university feels this way. Some do, of course, particularly if they are foreign nationals from a region where the local culture is very different. Most members of minority populations don't feel quite as isolated as the scenario depicted above. But many do feel at least some sense of isolation or "otherness." An important part of retaining these highly valued members of the college community, therefore, is to make it clear that they are indeed valued members of the community and their differences are not detriments, as far as the institution is concerned, but assets.

Academic leaders are often aware of the isolation that minority faculty members experience, but their efforts to address that isolation, although well intentioned, are sometimes ineffective. For instance, they may assume that the sense of community these faculty members long for involves only other minority faculty members. But merely because people are members of minority groups, it's not a given that they have other interests and outlooks in common. Artificially created social events intended solely or primarily for people from minority groups are thus unlikely to have the effect their organizers hoped for.

Instead what academic leaders can do is to be more effective in informing faculty members about the options that are available to them. They can ask recently hired faculty members what their interests are, what information about the community they want, and if there are individuals or groups that the faculty members would like to meet. Helping newcomers understand the resources that are available to them is usually much more effective than making assumptions about what minority faculty members—or, for that matter, *any* faculty member—wants and needs.

Academic leaders can also be candid in the assessment of the working environment in their department, college/division, or institution. Over time many people stop noticing troubling behavior because they've lived with it for so long. But Kerry Ann Rockquemore, president of the National Center for Faculty Development & Diversity, says that it's important for administrators to conduct an inventory of interpersonal practices periodically, asking such questions as

> Is there a department bully (or bullies)? Do packs of faculty collectively dismiss and demean pre-tenure faculty members publicly? Are there open secrets that are tolerated (Professor X is always drunk, Professor Y sexually harasses grad students or Professor Z yells and threatens people)? And if there are such things that everyone knows, why are they allowed? And more important, what are you willing to do about it? (Rockquemore, 2016)

Dismissing poor behavior among the faculty by saying things like, "Oh, that's just how Professor So-and-so is. He's really harmless." can significantly increase faculty attrition. *You* may have become used to Professor So-and-so's rude behavior, but the faculty member you're trying to retain may have not.

AVOID CULTURAL TAXATION

Another well-intentioned but ultimately harmful practice academic leaders engage in is something that Stanford education professor Amado Padilla has termed *cultural taxation*. Here's how it works.

An institution attempts to diversify its faculty and thus hires a group of minority faculty members. Because it values the perspectives of these faculty members, it includes them on its most important committees. Then, to make sure that additional candidates from minority groups receive due consideration for employment, it requires that all search committees be diversified. The result is that the service load of faculty members from minority groups ends up being significantly higher than that of other professors.

The problem with this kind of cultural taxation isn't merely that it increases the workload of minority faculty members; it's that it *shifts* the workload. More hours spent on search committees and in other service work means fewer hours conducting research, preparing for courses, and mentoring students. Since most colleges and universities weigh achievements in teaching and research far higher than they do achievements in service, this shift of responsibilities places minority faculty members at a disadvantage when decisions are made about promotion, tenure, and merit increases. As Patricia Matthew, associate professor of English at Montclair State University, explains,

> Those . . . who pay attention to diversity in higher education call [cultural taxation] "invisible labor"—not because no one sees it but because institutions don't value it with the currency they typically use to reward faculty work: reappointment, tenure, and promotion. Chances are a faculty member of color is not going to get a sabbatical or a grant from her institution because she contributes to the diversity mission her university probably has posted somewhere on its website. She certainly isn't going to get tenure for it. (Matthew, 2016)

Cultural taxation thus presents minority faculty members with a dilemma. Most college professors sincerely wish to do what is best for their institutions and the academic world as a whole. Minority faculty members are often eager to serve on search committees in order to help the institution diversify further. At the same time, however, the implicit message that "we're asking you to serve on this committee, not because you're good, but because you're a member of a minority group" can leave these faculty members feeling "used." That feeling is only exacerbated when these faculty members are routinely asked to provide the black/Latinx/transgender/women's perspective on issues, reinforcing the notion that they're regarded not as a professor but as a "[FILL IN THE BLANK WITH THE NAME OF THE APPROPRIATE GROUP] professor."

No group is monolithic. And it can be frustrating to be asked repeatedly to present perspectives "on behalf of" a specific gender or ethnic group. Like all professors, professors who are members of minority populations want to be seen as individuals and respected for their own contributions, not because of who they happen to "represent."

Colleges and universities can go a long way, therefore, if they stop asking themselves, "How can we better retain our black/Latinx/transgender/female faculty members?" and start asking, "How can we better retain *this* faculty member?" regardless of gender or ethnicity. If they do so, they'll stop the practice of cultural taxation, creating unfair burdens for members of minority groups in a well-intentioned effort to diversify their committees.

BEST PRACTICES AT EXEMPLARY INSTITUTIONS

One of the most comprehensive guides on how to retain minority faculty members was produced by the provost's office at Columbia University. Many of the suggestions presented in this guide are useful in the retention of all faculty members, not only those from minority populations. Among the useful recommendations presented in Columbia's guide are the following:

- Since each faculty member's needs are different, consider the use of leaves, dual-career accommodations, and other institutional resources that may help a faculty member address a personal issue while still remaining employed by the university.
- Provide faculty members with training in cultural sensitivity so as to avoid inadvertent statements, actions, and microaggressions that may make minority faculty members feel isolated or underappreciated.
- Conduct regular surveys to address morale and job satisfaction. These surveys should be conducted multiple times throughout the academic year since they provide only "snapshot" views of faculty sentiment at the moment when they are conducted. Take active measures to address areas of concern arising from these surveys.
- Disaggregate the data collected in these surveys so that programs measure morale, job satisfaction, and employee engagement by race or ethnicity, gender, discipline, length of service at the institution, career stage, and academic rank or role.
- Consider conducting focus groups of faculty members that can explore areas of satisfaction and dissatisfaction in greater detail.
- Monitor workload regularly to make sure that assignments are equitable.
- Monitor funding allocations to make sure that resources are fairly distributed.

- Simplify procedures wherever possible to prevent faculty members from having to devote excessive time to logistical matters like reimbursement for travel, textbook orders, office relocations, and the like.
- Conduct regular reviews of departmental practices so that there can be proactive responses to potential problems rather than reactive responses to actual problems.
- Examine the ways in which exit interviews are conducted to ensure that they provide meaningful insights into why faculty members are leaving and are not *pro forma* exercises performed merely to meet a requirement.
- Review evaluation criteria for processes like promotion, tenure, and merit salary increases to better align standards with what faculty members today are actually required to do.
- Provide opportunities for faculty members to meet both formally and informally as a way of building stronger community ties. (Office of the Provost, 2018)

Another institution that has developed a detailed plan for the retention of minority faculty members is the University of California, Davis (UC Davis). Regarding the issue of retaining a diverse faculty as integral to its goal of recruiting and retaining a diverse student body, UC Davis has developed an initiative that it calls CAMPOS: the Center for the Advancement of Multicultural Perspectives on Science. Complementing the ADVANCE Program, funded by grants from the National Science Foundation at many colleges and universities, CAMPOS is a systematic effort to provide career advancement to minority faculty members through mentoring, support of dual-career families, and conducting research into ways of breaking down barriers many minority faculty members face when pursuing a career in the sciences.

CAMPOS Scholars at UC Davis form a community that can provide mutual support and assistance. In addition, the program creates

> visibility for CAMPOS faculty scholars individually, collectively, locally, nationally, and internationally. CAMPOS hosts an induction ceremony each year to welcome, recognize its newest faculty scholars, and to disseminate their accomplishments. . . . [Opportunities available through CAMPOS also include] leadership skills development through the leadership institute, and programming to support regular networking to share common experiences, deliberate potential team science from interdisciplinary perspectives, and discuss issues of common concern through the Cafecitos (coffee gatherings) and celebratory dinners. (CAMPOS, 2020)

But CAMPOS isn't the only initiative UC Davis has taken to help retain its minority faculty members. It also partners extensively across the University of California System "to exchange and recruit diverse graduate and professional students, postdoctoral scholars and other academics for new tenure track faculty positions" (Pipeline, Recruitment, and Retention, 2017). It provides release time and other incentives for faculty members to engage in activities that might promote and retain minority scholars. It maintains advisory groups that can inform the institution about better ways to serve its minority community. And it seeks ways to approach diversity and inclusion training not as a separate objective but as a standard operating procedure that is embedded in a wide variety of activities from the institutional all the way down to the departmental level.

Promoting the retention of minority faculty members need not require the resources of a Columbia or a UC Davis. Smaller schools can develop centers that serve as advocacy centers and clearinghouses for resources related to multiculturalism, the unique needs of the LGBTQIA+ community, faculty members with disabilities, and other populations in an effort to promote inclusion and equity. Moreover, it costs nothing at all for academic leaders to initiate a discussion about how better to serve the needs of minority faculty members and to create a campus environment that values the talents and perspectives of each individual.

SUPPORTING MINORITY FACULTY MEMBERS

Larissa Mercado-Lopez, an associate professor of women's studies at California State University, Fresno, also suggests one obvious, but often overlooked strategy for retaining faculty members from minority groups: If you want to retain faculty members of color, support them *as* faculty members of color. What Mercado-Lopez means is that more needs to be done to develop infrastructure to support all the types of research and scholarship that members of minority groups do.

No one would suggest that minority faculty members *only* conduct research into topics related to race, gender, and ethnicity. There are minority chemists, mathematicians, European historians, philosophers, and accountants who rarely if ever give a single thought to these issues in their scholarship. But the fact remains that members of minority groups do have a unique perspective on their experiences that members of the majority group may understand intellectually, but can never undergo themselves. The distinctive voice of minority scholars thus brings a critical element to the academic world's pursuit of knowledge and needs support in order to be heard.

Many critics of the slogan Black Lives Matter argued that the very term used to describe this movement was racist. Instead, people should proclaim that *All* Lives Matter. But the expression Black Lives Matter wasn't shorthand for *Only* Black Lives Matter. It was a reminder that Black Lives Matter, *Too*, at a time when the actions of certain authority figures seemed to have forgotten that fact. Mercado-Lopez suggests that too often the higher education response to minority retention is similarly All Faculty Matter when what colleges and universities need to understand is that Minority Faculty Matter, *Too*.

Supporting faculty members of color *as* faculty members of color means, as Mercado-Lopez concludes, that institutions of higher education need to provide more

> resources, institutional spaces, and leadership development opportunities specifically for faculty of color. . . . Often, faculty of color in search of identity-specific support are pointed to existing structures or asked to create their own spaces. These can look like faculty learning communities, faculty and staff organizations, or centers for cross-cultural student services that can offer resources and collaboration space to faculty. (Mercado-Lopez, 2018)

Those efforts, while valuable and well intentioned, aren't enough. Diversifying the hiring process takes more than an Equal Opportunity program where barriers to minority candidates are removed. It takes an Affirmative Action process where due consideration of qualified minority applicants is encouraged. In order to stem continued attrition of minority faculty members, institutions can't merely take an Equal Opportunity approach to support of scholarship. It has to take an Affirmative Action approach there as well.

As Mercado-Lopez concludes,

> Valuing faculty of color means changing the language about them from "having diverse perspectives" to "embodying critical knowledges," and being open to the ways that these faculty might unsettle current power structures. It means taking the risk of being critiqued by white faculty for being exclusionary. Importantly, it means responding to these critiques with the insistence that supporting faculty of color is a form of social and educational justice. (Mercado-Lopez, 2018)

In a report to the Council of Colleges of Arts and Sciences, Aldemaro Romero, dean of the Weissman School of Arts and Sciences at Baruch College, notes that the retention of minority faculty members must be part of a comprehensive diversity plan. Piecemeal efforts to stem attrition aren't effective in the long term. An overall strategy to promote diversity in hiring, development, and support of faculty members from minority groups is the only *sustainable* way to retain these members of the community and to increase their level of engagement with the institution (Romero, 2017).

Of course, taking the approach recommended by Mercado-Lopez, Romero, and others requires systemic changes that are often far beyond the ability of any department chair or member of a search committee to implement. That doesn't mean, however, that there aren't practical steps for academic leaders to take while they work on implementing those larger changes.

Romero notes, for example, that academic leaders can increase the visibility of scholarship produced by minority faculty members through instituting recognitions like a "Diversity Achievement Award every year based on nominations from faculty, staff, and students to recognize significant contributions in this area" (Romero, 2017). They can create multicultural resource directories. They can provide bridge funding to support research by minority faculty members or to diversify the faculty without waiting for current employees to retire or leave the institution for other reasons. They can focus part of their fundraising efforts on developing external resources to support faculty diversity. And they can expand their leadership development programs to include meaningful programs for women and members of minority groups (Romero, 2017).

CONCLUSION

Many of the strategies that increase the retention of all faculty members also increase the retention of minority faculty members and vice versa. But because of the challenges many minority faculty members face in the academic world—a feeling of isolation, well-intentioned but ultimately excessive service expectations, the impression conveyed by at least some of their peers that they didn't earn their positions or that their research is insignificant—academic leaders also have to take special steps in order to increase the retention of faculty members from minority groups. Otherwise many of them will be lured away by other institutions that are also seeking to diversify their staffs.

In summary, many colleges and universities do a great deal to attract qualified faculty members from minority groups but little or nothing to retain them. Others develop retention plans based on the assumption that academic leaders already know what these professors want without bothering to ask them. The best approach always tends to be one that consults with minority faculty members to find out what they need and want and then provides a range of options to meet those requirements and desires.

Attracting and retaining a diverse student body means that institutions of higher education have to attract and retain a diverse faculty. And hiring a diverse faculty also means institutions have to do everything they can to *retain* a diverse faculty. Those efforts have to begin with candid conversations about what is currently working, what isn't as effective as it could be, and what needs to be done in order to promote the success of professors the institution worked very hard to recruit in the first place.

KEY POINTS IN THIS CHAPTER

- Many of the approaches that are useful in retaining minority faculty members are also useful in retaining *all* faculty members.
- Many institutions devote significant resources to recruiting minority faculty members but fail to devote resources to supporting those faculty members once they hire them.
- Minority faculty members tend to persist at an institution when they are properly onboarded, given access to a mentor, assigned responsibilities that are adjusted if necessary to promote their success and truly reflective of the institution's mission and aspirations, and allocated a sufficient amount of support for research and socialization.
- Cultural taxation, the excessive assignment of minority faculty members to committees in a well-intentioned effort to obtain diversity, is a major obstacle to retention.
- When minority faculty members do leave an institution, their exit interviews should not be *pro forma* but should explore the full range of reasons why that professor chose not to stay.
- Regular cultural sensitivity training tends to reduce microaggressions and other remarks that minority faculty members find offensive so as to create a more open and welcoming environment for everyone.
- In order to retain minority faculty members, institutions should support them *as* minority faculty members.

REFERENCES

CAMPOS: UC Davis. (2020). https://diversity.ucdavis.edu/campos.

Matthew, P. A. (2016). What is faculty diversity worth to a university? *The Atlantic.* https://www.theatlantic.com/education/archive/2016/11/what-is-faculty-diversity-worth-to-a-university/508334/.

Mercado-Lopez, L. (2018). Want to retain faculty of color? Support them as faculty of color. *Medium.* https://medium.com/national-center-for-institutional-diversity/want-to-retain-faculty-of-color-support-them-as-faculty-of-color-9e7154ed618f.

Office of the Provost: Columbia University. (2018). *Guide* to best practices in faculty retention. https://provost.columbia.edu/sites/default/files/content/Faculty%20Diversity%20and%20Inclusion/BestPracticesFacultyRetention.pdf.

Pipeline, Recruitment, and Retention: UC Davis. (2017). https://diversity.ucdavis.edu/pipeline-recruitment-and-retention.

Rockquemore, K. A. (2016). For a diverse faculty, start with retention. *Inside Higher Ed.* https://www.insidehighered.com/advice/2016/01/06/how-retain-diverse-faculty-essay.

Romero, A. (2017). Best practices for recruiting and retaining diverse faculty for institutions of higher education. https://www.ccas.net/files/public/Publications/Best%20Practices%20CCAS_March%202017_FINAL.pdf.

RESOURCES

Aguirre, A. (2000). *Women and minority faculty in the academic workplace: Recruitment, retention, academic culture.* Washington, DC: ERIC Clearinghouse on Higher Education.

August, L., & Waltman, J. (2004). Culture, climate, and contribution: Career satisfaction among female faculty. *Research in Higher Education.* 45(2), 177–192.

Burgoyne, R., Shaw, T. M., Dawson, R. C., & Scheinkman, R. (2010). *Navigating a complex landscape to foster greater faculty and student diversity in higher education.* Washington, DC: American Association for the Advancement of Science.

Chun, E., & Evans, A. (2015). *The department chair as transformative diversity leader: Building inclusive learning environments in higher education.* Sterling, VA: Stylus.

Gasman, M. (2010). Ten ways to retain faculty of color. *Diverse Issues in Higher Education.* https://diverseeducation.com/article/31272/.

Gasman, M., Kim, J., & Nguyen, T. (2011). Effectively recruiting faculty of color at highly selective institutions: A school of education case study. *Journal of Diversity in Higher Education.* 4(4), 212–222.

Kline, M. (2018). Underpaid and underrepresented: Women of color in the higher ed workforce. *The Higher Ed Workplace Blog.* https://www.cupahr.org/blog/underpaid-and-underrepresented-women-of-color-in-the-higher-ed-workforce/.

Moody, J. A. (2012). *Faculty diversity: Removing the barriers.* New York, NY: Routledge.

Rosser, V. J. (2004). Faculty members' intentions to leave: A national study on their worklife and satisfaction. *Research in Higher Education.* 45(3), 285–309.

Social Sciences Feminist Network Research Interest Group: University of Oregon. (2017). The burden of invisible work in academia: Social inequalities and time use in five university departments. *Humboldt Journal of Social Relations.* 39(1), 228–235.

Chapter 3

Best Practices in Onboarding and Orientation

One of the most uncomfortable truths for academic leaders to realize is that they lose many of their best faculty members long before they know they're in danger of losing them. Think of your first day of work as you began an academic position. Weren't you excited (and maybe a little nervous) about the opportunities that lay ahead? Weren't you grateful to the institution for offering you the position? Weren't you committed to doing your best?

But then what happened after you arrived? The precise stages in the onboarding and orientation process will probably differ from institution to institution, but they may have included some or all of the following:

- Being forced to complete an orientation "death march" where you were led painfully and slowly through reams of institutional policies, information about benefits, and forms to complete until your eyes glazed over
- Being handed a stack of brochures and manuals to read, which you probably never read and which may even now be cluttering up a shelf somewhere
- Being required to complete online training about sexual harassment, multicultural sensitivity, research ethics, and other topics that, while undeniably important, were probably presented in as dull a manner as possible
- Being taken around and introduced to dozens of people, none of whose names you could possibly remember by the end of the day

Didn't all of that make you lose some of your enthusiasm for your new position? Think of it this way: If instead of during your first day on the job you'd been treated that way on your first date with someone, would you ever have agreed to a second date?

In their book *The Power of Moments*, Chip and Dan Heath talk about the importance of the first day someone spends at work as a *time of transition* (Heath and Heath, 2017, 17–22). Transitions are those key experiences everyone has that cause them to think ever afterward in times of "the time before them" and "the time after them." People speak in this way all the time: "Back before I went to college . . ." or "Once we had our first child . . .". Few industries handle the transition of an employee to a new job well. Higher education handles it abominably.

The Heath brothers contrast the approach taken by most companies to that taken by the John Deere Company. Shorty after someone accepts a job at John Deere, that person receives a letter from a current employee. The letter welcomes the new employee, explains where to park, what the company dress code is, and a few other details that someone would need to know right away.

On the new employee's first day at work, he or she is met in the lobby by the same person who wrote the letter. Monitors welcome the new employee by name. The new employee is taken to the place where he or she will work and discovers a welcome banner there. The first email message the new employee receives is from the company's CEO, explaining the mission of the John Deere Company and hoping that the person's day goes well.

At noon, the person is taken to lunch by a small group of coworkers, including the person who had written the welcome letter. Before the day ends, the new employee's "big boss" (i.e., his or her supervisor's supervisor) stops by to schedule a lunch in the near future. There's also a small gift on the employee's desk (see Heath and Heath, 2017, 20–21).

To rephrase the question raised earlier, if instead of what you experienced during your first day on the job you'd been treated on your first date with someone in the way just outlined by Chip and Dan Heath, would you have agreed to a second date? Chances are very high that you would. But the problem is that the John Deere "First Day Experience" is almost the exact opposite of how most colleges and universities treat faculty members when they start work.

Faculty orientation activities usually try to cram too much information into too short a period of time, are boring, and fail to focus on matters that the professoriate really cares about (academic freedom, tenure, and research support). Instead they focus on matters that human resource directors tend to care about (policies, benefits, and paperwork), draining new faculty members of some of their enthusiasm from the very start.

As Columbia University's *Guide to Best Practices in Faculty Retention* explains, "Orientations for new faculty are a good starting point, but fall privy to being too much too soon and are not enough to help new faculty acclimate to their new community" (Office of the Provost, 2018). In order to create environments that are more likely to lead to faculty retention, colleges and universities should consider replacing their current onboarding and orientation efforts with two alternatives: a Faculty First Day Welcome and a Faculty First Year Experience.

THE FACULTY FIRST DAY WELCOME

One of the mistakes commonly made in higher education involves the compartmentalization of knowledge. A discovery is made in one area but its relevance elsewhere may remain long unrealized. Among academic leaders, this type of compartmentalization can occur when we recognize important principles about the recruitment and retention of students but fail to apply those principles to the recruitment and retention of faculty.

For example, administrators learned long ago that the onboarding of students needed to convey the feeling that the institution was glad they were there and committed to their success. As strange as it may seem now, it wasn't very long ago where, at large orientation assemblies, the president or a dean would say to the incoming students, "Look to the right of you. Look to the left of you. By the start of the second semester, one of the three of you will no longer be here." The idea was to convey the impression that college was serious business. Those who didn't work hard enough wouldn't succeed. And the school wasn't there to "hold students' hands"; it was there to serve as a gatekeeper that prevented those who weren't smart enough or hardworking enough from calling themselves college graduates.

Once colleges became more dependent on the revenue generated by tuition and student credit hour production, they stopped presenting themselves as indifferent to student success and began to act in a more welcoming manner. Onboarding ceased its emphasis on how hard college will be and shifted its focus to how fun college would be. Batteries of placement tests were replaced by series of social events. The message became, "We're glad you're here and will do everything in our power to help you achieve your goals."

Institutions also became increasingly clever about the types of experiences they provided. Large universities can sometimes make students feel as though they're anonymous faces in a crowd. Small colleges can make students feel as though they are missing out on the excitement of a large campus. So, larger schools would frequently break students into small groups and require "freshman seminars" with limited enrollment as a way of building a sense of community. Smaller schools began conducting orientation activities with all incoming students at once and requiring "College 101" classes where students would get the sense that they were part of a larger enterprise.

Nevertheless, few of these insights were transferred to the onboarding of faculty. Although there might be a welcome dinner or reception, most onboarding activities were focused on completing paperwork and outlining the standards new faculty members would have to complete in order to earn promotion and tenure. For the sake of efficiency, these sessions were often conducted with all new faculty members at once. Although the intention may have been to be helpful, the tone these sessions conveyed was about as unwelcoming as could be imagined.

Transferring the lessons learned about retaining students to the retention of faculty would look something like this. The moment of transition that colleges and universities handle the best is probably graduation. Decades—sometimes centuries—of commencement exercises have caused school to master the art of how to make these important moments in the lives of their students memorable. There are, of course, both idealistic and commercial reasons for doing so. On the level of ideals, graduation becomes a time for the academic community to regenerate itself, acknowledging the next generation of scholars that will carry its name. On a strictly commercial level, those graduates are now alumni, and alumni are more likely to contribute generously to their alma maters if they have pleasant moments of communal experience to look back on.

So, schools do everything in their power to make graduation a special event. The campus is beautified. Regalia is brought out. Awards are presented. Ceremonies are performed. To make the event seem more personal, some larger schools schedule more intimate ceremonies within the colleges as well as mass ceremonies for the institution as a whole. Every effort is made to make this moment of transition seem as special as possible.

Why isn't that same creativity applied to the Faculty First Day Welcome? Instead of paperwork and dull training sessions, the welcome event should be characterized by academic grandeur. Current faculty as well as those newly hired should dress in regalia, and regalia should be rented for them if they don't already own it. Rather than signing lengthy forms, new faculty members should sign their names in a large, ornate book, indicating that they're entering the ranks of the professoriate. A large convocation of all the faculty should be complemented with smaller, more personal events on the college, department, or even personal level to send the message that the new member of the community is valued as an individual and that his or her colleagues embrace their new coworkers as equals.

The message conveyed throughout these events should be that the institution will do everything in its power to make the new faculty member successful. Each of the new professors should meet with a mentor who will underscore the school's commitment to faculty achievement. At the end of the day, the new faculty members should feel valued, energized, and committed to bringing their excitement into their teaching, research, and service. They should look back on their first day as both meaningful and fun.

And what of all that necessary paperwork that has to be done? What about the processing of identification cards, parking permits, and forms acknowledging the receipt of keys, policy manuals, and benefits brochures? All of that can still be done—just not on the first day. A vast amount of onboarding paperwork can be completed by new faculty members even before they arrive in town. In fact, the completion of paperwork can be converted from a mind-numbing ordeal to a strategy for building excitement for the start of a new academic year.

Most faculty members are now hired weeks and even months before the school year begins. If critical paperwork is parceled out instead of collected into a single packet, accompanied by letters of welcome from various campus offices, and stretched out over the period from the signing of the contract to the Faculty First Day Welcome, it builds a sense of purpose. It makes it feel as though the faculty member is moving *toward* a goal rather than faced with a huge obstacle before the journey even begins.

Other paperwork can be completed as needed over the next few days, weeks, or even months. That's where the next component of what colleges and universities can learn from the student experience comes in. New professors need a Faculty First Year Experience.

THE FACULTY FIRST YEAR EXPERIENCE

Another lesson that colleges and universities have learned from working with students is that short, highly condensed orientation sessions aren't effective. Not that long ago "freshman orientation" was a relatively brief affair. New students would arrive on campus a few days before classes began and—in addition to the common "Look to the right of you. Look to the left of you." speech and endless placement exams—were shown where the library was and, if they were lucky, where their first class would meet.

But as colleges and universities became more student friendly, they learned that this type of orientation wasn't just unwelcoming; it was also highly inadequate. Incoming students were bombarded with so much information in such a short time that they couldn't possibly retain it. By the end of the first term when they actually had final exams, everything they'd learned months earlier about the school's final exam policy had been forgotten. By the time they had to register for their second term's courses, the procedure they'd used to register during the first term no longer seemed familiar.

Information overload prevents people from learning effectively. Incoming students were still adjusting to life on campus rather than at home and trying to find a new circle of friends that would become their social network. Many of the policies and procedures they learned during orientation became lost in the haze. For this reason, most schools either replaced or supplemented their highly condensed "freshman orientations" with a First Year Experience: an extended period during which students could make the transition to college life gradually and where they could receive the information they needed in a "just-in-time" manner rather than all at once.

If colleges and universities learned that this approach leads to better *student* retention, why don't they understand that a similar approach will lead to better *faculty* retention? Schools that are serious about improving the retention of their best professors ought to consider implementing a Faculty First Year Experience.

What would a Faculty First Year Experience be? It would be a structured program that would begin with the Faculty First Day Welcome mentioned earlier and continue through commencement at the end of the year. Throughout this time, new faculty members would receive information only when they needed it so that they could absorb it more gradually. They'd also get together regularly with other first year faculty members with the result that they'd build a stronger sense of community at the institution beyond their immediate departments.

Each institution's Faculty First Year Experience would be designed based on that school's individual mission and vision. But as a template of possible topics to cover, the following might serve as an initial guide.

August

- Faculty First Day Welcome

September

- Teaching Focus: Teaching large classes
- Research Focus: The role and function of the IRB (Institutional Review Board)
- Service Focus: Committee structure at the institution
- Policy Focus: Intercultural sensitivity

October

- Teaching Focus: Best practices in online teaching
- Research Focus: Services provided by the division/office of research
- Service Focus: Balancing service with teaching and research responsibilities
- Policy Focus: How the budget works

November

- Teaching Focus: Strategies for consistent evaluation of student work
- Research Focus: Developing a research agenda
- Service Focus: Selecting your first service role
- Policy Focus: Sexual harassment, sexual misconduct, and the workplace

December

- Teaching Focus: Dealing with student grade appeals
- Research Focus: A deep dive into research integrity
- Service Focus: How the faculty senate/assembly works
- Policy Focus: First-term retrospective, "How did it go?"

January

- Teaching Focus: The Socratic method
- Research Focus: Applying for external grants
- Service Focus: How curriculum proposals are approved
- Policy Focus: The institutional travel policy

February

- Teaching Focus: Additional strategies for active learning
- Research Focus: Developing budgets for research projects
- Service Focus: Service to the discipline
- Policy Focus: The outside employment/activities policy

March

- Teaching Focus: The professor as mentor and role model
- Research Focus: Local resources for writing assistance related to articles, books, grant proposals, and other research-related activities
- Service Focus: Service to the institution
- Policy Focus: The summer teaching policy

April

- Teaching Focus: Developing and assigning capstone projects
- Research Focus: Strategies and methods for solo research
- Service Focus: Service to the community
- Policy Focus: The records retention and disposition policy

May

- Teaching Focus: Teaching with technology
- Research Focus: Strategies and methods for team-based research
- Service Focus: Documenting service achievements
- Policy Focus: Applying for promotion, "What first year faculty members need to know *now*"

Should these sessions be required or merely encouraged? The answer to that question will depend on the mission and traditions of the school but, at the very least, supervisors might suggest that they *expect* their new faculty members to attend and participate in as much of this program as possible.

The goal would be for each of these monthly or biweekly sessions to combine both social and informational elements. It's not effective to prepare a faculty to promote active learning by their students if the faculty development program itself consists of a series of dry lectures. The sessions should be structured in such a way that the participants have ample time to mingle, get to know one another, and build their social networks. When information is shared, it should be shared in an engaging manner, with exercises, inventories, and case studies, not just PowerPoint slides.

Case studies, in particular, work well in these sessions. They provide new faculty members with an opportunity to think through how they'd handle various kinds of challenges and take advantage of various kinds of opportunities. They make policies more meaningful by seeing the implications of those policies in realistic situations, not merely as theoretical constructs. (See Siddiqui, Papanagnou, Bruno, and Novielli, 2019.) Best of all, they give the administrators in charge of the Faculty First Year Experience program an opportunity to "flip the classroom."

It would be difficult to find an academic professional today who's not familiar with the *flipped classroom*, that educational strategy in which facts and formulae that used to be presented inside the classroom are now distributed through videos and resources of the classroom management system outside the class. Doing so leaves more time for students to process and synthesize information in class through experiments, discussions, and other activities.

Yet again it seems appropriate to ask: If these techniques are already known to increase student retention, why aren't they being applied to the challenge of faculty retention? College professors are bright people. They can *read* a policy; they don't need to be force-marched through it with a dull presentation.

Some administrators will object, "But it's making a very big assumption to say that faculty members will read materials in advance. They won't. No one actually reads materials before meetings." That will be true in certain cases, of course. Nevertheless, people tend to live up or down to whatever expectations you place on them. If you tell new faculty members that they're expected to read the material, most of them will, particularly if you explain that the alternative is a long, very dull meeting where they are told information they could easily have read on their own.

By distributing policy statements and other written materials well in advance of the session and then devoting meeting time to seeing why that information is relevant to new faculty members through role plays and other active learning techniques, the Faculty First Year Experience transforms the orientation process from one that destroys enthusiasm to one that builds faculty engagement. (For more on the Faculty First Year Experience, see Buller, 2012, 267–273.)

THE ROLE OF CLUSTER HIRING IN RETENTION

Cluster hiring—the practice of simultaneously hiring a group of scholars with related research interests—has become a common practice in higher education. It allows schools to establish specialty areas almost overnight and has been proven effective in creating increased diversity (see Flaherty, 2015). But what is sometimes overlooked is the role that cluster hiring can play in increasing faculty retention.

As was noted earlier, a major benefit that arises from the Faculty First Day Welcome and the Faculty First Year Experience, when these activities are designed properly, is their ability to create a sense of community and team spirit among those who have been recently hired. Cluster hiring takes this approach one step further by creating a group with an *instant* sense of community since they all share a group identity from the very beginning.

The University of Wisconsin–Madison, where faculty retention has been a challenge (see Chapter 1) and where the formal practice of cluster hiring began in 1998, uses the practice to provide new research tracks and collaborative opportunities; bring additional areas of research distinction to the university; increase campus diversity; promote interdisciplinary cooperation; and remove barriers to faculty retention, such as the problem of finding meaningful employment for dual-career families.

Although to date there has not yet been sufficient statistical analysis of cluster hiring's impact, anecdotal evidence does suggest that it does improve faculty retention (Flaherty, 2015; and Walker, 2020). Susan D. Phillips, senior vice president for academic affairs at State University of New York Downstate Medical Center and vice president for strategic partnerships at SUNY Albany, notes that "cluster hiring programs live and die by how supported they are once the new faculty members are on campus" (Flaherty, 2015). As was the case with retention of minority faculty members, investment in cluster hiring can't be limited to "the front end." Ongoing support and development of faculty members who were hired as part of a cluster continues to be necessary if these retention efforts are to succeed.

In short, therefore, cluster hiring cannot be seen as *the* answer to faculty retention. But, coupled with the other approaches discussed in this chapter, it can be part of *an* answer. It can be a step in the direction of providing greater community and building esprit de corps, both of which encourage faculty members to stay when they are present and cause attrition to increase when they diminish.

CONCLUSION

The time to start thinking about faculty retention isn't when valued members of the community threaten to leave. It's at the very moment of their hiring. In fact, faculty retention efforts should begin even *before* professors are hired by asking questions about what sort of community culture new recruits will be joining, how they will be socialized into that community, and how they will be supported throughout their careers.

Currently, colleges and universities generally do a rather poor job of making new faculty members feel welcome and of providing them with the information they need to succeed when they need it and not in an overburdened "Day of Welcome." The Faculty First Day Welcome, Faculty First Year Experience, and cluster hiring are all tools that every school should have in its toolkit if it intends to make a serious effort at faculty retention. But even these tools alone are not enough. There also needs to be a consistent program of faculty support and development at other critical stages in a faculty member's career. And that will be the focus of the next chapter.

KEY POINTS IN THIS CHAPTER

- Many problems with faculty retention begin at the point of onboarding and orientation.
- Colleges and universities should apply the lessons they learned about how best to bring new students into the community to their processes of onboarding new faculty members.
- A Faculty First Day Welcome should not be a dull event, filled with speeches, paperwork, and policy manuals, but should make newly hired professors excited about and engaged with the community.

- A Faculty First Year Experience should provide the information that new faculty members need in a "just-in-time" fashion that parcels out these details over the course of several months.
- The Faculty First Year Experience should also give professors a chance to socialize and build their personal networks.
- In addition to diversifying the faculty and providing areas of research excellence, cluster hiring can also be used to promote faculty retention.

REFERENCES

Buller, J. L. (2012). *The essential department chair: A comprehensive desk reference* (2nd ed.). San Francisco, CA: Jossey-Bass.

Flaherty, C. (2015). Cluster hiring and diversity. *Inside Higher Ed.* https://www.insidehighered.com/news/2015/05/01/new-report-says-cluster-hiring-can-lead-increased-faculty-diversity.

Heath, C., & Heath, D. (2017). *The power of moments: Why certain experiences have extraordinary impact.* New York, NY: Simon & Schuster.

Office of the Provost: Columbia University. (2018). *Guide* to best practices in faculty retention. https://provost.columbia.edu/sites/default/files/content/Faculty%20Diversity%20and%20Inclusion/BestPracticesFacultyRetention.pdf.

Siddiqui, M., Papanagnou, D., Bruno, S., & Novielli, K. (2019). The case for revamping new faculty orientation: Integrating case-based learning into faculty onboarding. *Mededportal. 15*(1). https://www.ncbi.nlm.nih.gov/pmc/articles/PMC6944263/.

Walker, S. (2020). The untapped potential of 'cluster hiring.' *The Wall Street Journal.* https://www.wsj.com/articles/a-business-lesson-from-academia-great-teams-assemble-themselves-11578718805.

RESOURCES

Clark, T., Corral, J., Nyberg, E., Bang, T., Trivedi, P., Sachs, P., Mcarthur, T., . . . Rumack, C. (2018). Launchpad for onboarding new faculty into academic life. *Current Problems in Diagnostic Radiology. 47*(2), 72–74.

Cullen, R., & Harris, M. (2008). Supporting new scholars: A learner-centered approach to new faculty orientation. *Florida Journal of Educational Administration & Policy. 2*(1), 17–28.

Eisner, S. (2015). Onboarding the faculty: A model for win-win mentoring. *American Journal of Business Education. 8*(1), 7–22.

Piercy, F., Giddings, V., Allen, K., Dixon, B., Meszaros, P., & Joest, K. (2005). Improving campus climate to support faculty diversity and retention: A pilot program for new faculty. *Innovative Higher Education. 30*(1), 53–66.

Chapter 4

Providing Support at Critical Points

The American essayist Charles Dudley Warner is almost forgotten today, but he originated a famous observation that's commonly misattributed to Mark Twain: "Everybody complains about the weather, but nobody does anything about it." The academic equivalent of this remark might be, "Everyone believes in faculty development, but no one really knows what it is."

It's not that academic leaders don't *think* they know what faculty development is. It's just that if you examine their efforts to develop their faculty members it becomes immediately clear that most of them have very little idea how to do it effectively. They may have a fund to send people to conferences and consider that to constitute their effort at faculty development. They may support a workshop every now and then on such topics as how to apply for promotion or how to teach an online course. And they may even put together a series about issues they think faculty members should care about.

But is any of that really faculty development? And if it is, is that *all* that the expression *faculty development* means?

Certainly there are organizations that can assist academic leaders with their efforts in this area. For example, the POD Network specifically aims to help institutions move beyond programs that merely help faculty members become better teachers to programs that deal with the full range of what college professors do today. But not enough chairs, deans, and provosts avail themselves of the opportunities provided by the POD Network. They leave that instead to the directors of their teaching and learning centers or a faculty liaison officer.

And who can blame them? Academic leaders today are expected to be student recruiters, fundraisers, assessment officers, hiring agents, mentors, counselors, and a host of other things besides. So, it's no wonder that their efforts at faculty development are either haphazard, delegated to others, or both. The problem is that poor faculty development can result in poor faculty retention.

So, as difficult as it is, academic leaders have to rethink their commitment to how they develop the faculty members they worked so hard to hire.

WHAT IS FACULTY DEVELOPMENT?

Faculty development consists of everything an institution does to maintain and enhance its faculty members in their diverse and evolving roles. It's not just instructional development. It's not just research development. It's not just helping faculty members understand and adhere to institutional policies. It's all that and more.

While providing faculty development opportunities can be a fairly complex process, deciding what faculty development is can be quite simple. You merely need to answer two questions:

1. What do faculty members do in my program (or at my institution)?
2. What training, resources, and other support can I provide to help them do those things better?

The reason why faculty development programs don't always increase retention is that too many academic leaders don't go far enough in answering these questions. They either identify faculty development with improvement of instruction; don't identify faculty responsibilities beyond the standard academic triad of teaching, research, and service; or don't think creatively enough about the types of training, resources, and other support that might be possible.

Consider, for instance, how the faculty role has expanded over the years. Earlier it was noted that academic leaders today are expected to engage in student recruitment, fundraising, outcomes assessment, and many other activities that chairs, deans, and provosts weren't formerly required to do. But faculty members are also expected to take on responsibilities in those areas. If full-time administrators feel unprepared to succeed at these new roles, how much less do faculty members feel ready for them at the same time that they're preparing their courses, publishing their research, and serving on the ever-expanding number of committees and task forces that characterize the modern university?

On a website titled "What Do Faculty Do?" the American Association of University Professors lists *thirty* different responsibilities commonly assigned to college professors these days. Those responsibilities include

- counseling students about personal problems, learning difficulties, or life choices,

- writing letters of recommendation to help students enter graduate programs or secure jobs or internships,
- evaluating a colleague's work for promotion or tenure,
- participating in a departmental self-study,
- and many other activities as well (What Do Faculty Do? n.d.).

Yet, despite all these expectations, how many colleges and universities train their faculty members in counseling, writing effective letters of recommendation, evaluating the credential's of their colleagues, or reviewing programs objectively?

Even worse, when faculty development *is* provided, it usually adopts the philosophy that "one size fits all." The assumption is that the beginning instructor and the distinguished professor have identical needs in terms of learning about technology, applying for grants, improving student writing, taking on leadership roles, and whatever else the typical faculty development series might address. But the fact is that the needs of college professors change significantly over the course of their careers, and a critical component of improving faculty retention is to provide the right kind of support at critical points in each person's professional growth.

WHAT NEWER FACULTY MEMBERS WANT AND NEED

In the first stage of a college professor's career, which might be defined as the years leading up to applying for promotion to the rank of associate professor, both time and money are extremely precious resources. Money tends to be scarce because these are the years when a faculty member's income is usually the lowest. Time tends to be scarce because if the faculty member fails to qualify for promotion by the institution's deadline his or her contract is not renewed.

Those two scarce resources, time and money, can trap newer faculty members in a vicious circle. Because their income is low, they often volunteer to teach overloads and summer courses. But these opportunities to increase income require an investment of time that could have been spent on research or preparing their courses. So, their work-life balance suffers as time that could have been spent with family and friends or devoted to soul-nurturing recreational pursuits must now be redirected toward professional obligations. Relationships sometimes suffer during this period of a faculty member's life, and if a marriage ends or a cohabiting couple splits up, the financial strain becomes even more severe, and the vicious circle continues.

Along with all the personal and professional damage this situation can create, faculty attrition can increase. Otherwise promising faculty members may not be granted tenure or long-term contracts because of insufficient research. Professional burnout can cause even those who *do* qualify for tenure or long-term contracts to seek positions elsewhere. The "one-size-fits-all" faculty development approach doesn't work because many of the opportunities that colleges and universities provide require the further investment of time (to attend workshops and complete online training) and money (to absorb the portion of conference expenses not subsidized by the institution), the very resources that newer faculty members have in short supply anyway.

What newer college professors want and need, therefore, are faculty development resources that do four things simultaneously. First, they should lay a solid foundation for the rest of the faculty member's career. Second, they should require only a minimal investment of time. Third, they should include financial incentives whenever possible. And fourth, they should increase the faculty member's level of engagement with the institution.

Accomplishing these goals often requires colleges and universities to rethink the faculty development opportunities they provide. For example, if the institution is offering a workshop that it regards as vital to a newer faculty member's professional development, is it also offering daycare accommodations so that a faculty member with young children can attend? Is it structuring those programs to be as respectful of the faculty member's time as possible?

Is it offering financial incentives, such as a stipend for completing a training program about online learning or Title IX, so that those with limited resources are encouraged to participate? Is it scheduling its programs at a time of day that doesn't create problems for those who have to pick up children from school or prepare meals? Is it expecting that the faculty members pay for the programs they're required to attend?

Too many faculty development programs fail to answer these questions. They're designed by people who don't face the same challenges that newer faculty members face and so don't consider the issues that can create obstacles for the very people the programs are intended to serve.

Moreover, as will be illustrated below, the sort of career advice and development that newer faculty members need is often very different from the sort of career advice and development that college professors need when they are already well established. Newer faculty members aren't yet concerned about their legacies; they're concerned with keeping their jobs (and, in many cases, with paying off student loans). For this reason, a faculty development program that both gives these employees the support they need and introduces them to the hard truths they need to hear (but that others too often fail to tell them) will help them the most.

One of these hard truths is that newer faculty members need to be very selective about their service commitments. It can take a long time to get a grant proposal accepted or a book published. It can take years, sometimes even decades, before a professor is told "You changed my life" by a former student. But service commitments *appear* to have an immediate payoff. If you agree to serve on a committee, you can list that committee as one of your accomplishments *today*.

Newer faculty members thus often volunteer for too many committee assignments. They don't understand that the time required for these activities may be far out of proportion to the career benefits they provide. When they are being considered for promotion, their teaching is "graded." Their research is "graded." But most colleges and universities evaluate service largely on a "pass/fail" basis: Did the person do his or her fair share?

Near the beginning of their careers, faculty members are sometimes attracted to service commitments for other reasons, too. They may see them as a chance to meet other highly educated people from outside their departments. They may feel grateful for having been hired by the school and want to give back to it in some way. Those are certainly fine sentiments but, like fair words, fine sentiments "butter no parsnips."

Junior faculty members should be devoting a significant amount of time to preparing their courses, improving their instructional methods, advancing their research agendas, and disseminating their research results. Committee work doesn't do much to help newer faculty members accomplish those goals, and a good mentoring or development program should tell them so.

The second hard truth newer faculty members should learn is that they need a clear plan. The plan shouldn't be for the rest of their lives or even for the rest of their careers; it should be for the next five years. What have the portfolios of those faculty members who have recently become associate professors looked like? What were their scores on student course evaluations? How many articles did they publish? How many grant dollars did they bring in?

Student ratings, numbers of publications, and size of grants may indeed be a terrible way of measuring a faculty member's success, but those are the criteria that are used at most colleges and universities. If you're going to be evaluated by the numbers, you should at least know what those numbers are.

You should also have a plan for attaining them. If your scores on student course evaluations aren't what they should be, what's your strategy for raising them? How might a center for teaching and learning or a conference with sessions on improving pedagogy help? If you need to have published ten articles to be promoted, your goal should be to publish at least two articles a year. How have you blocked out the time you'll need to do so?

When should you complete each article? When should you begin? Which journals "count" the most in your field? What sorts of articles have they been accepting lately, and how might you need to adapt your research accordingly?

The newer faculty member's plan for the next five years is a strategy for getting promoted, but it's also a great deal more. It helps the person achieve greater work-life balance by parceling out objectives over time. The faculty member may have succeeded as a student by "cramming" for tests. But "cramming" for promotion rarely works, and it rarely produces much life satisfaction. Having a plan that indicates when different activities should begin, when they should end, and when various milestones should be achieved along the way can help the person not only succeed at the job, but also lead a fulfilling life. It can also indicate when taking on an overload course or summer program may be advisable, and when it may not.

The third hard truth that the faculty development program should reveal to newer faculty members is that they need to focus. They want to and should engage in all the aspects of being a full member of the higher education community, but they don't need to do them all *now*.

Building a foundation for the rest of a faculty member's career is easiest when the faculty member establishes a strong professional identity. It becomes significantly harder when the faculty member tries to become a superstar teacher *and* an internationally acclaimed researcher *and* an opinion leader among peers *and* a host of other things besides. Focusing on establishing a stellar research agenda now doesn't mean that one can't be recognized as "Adviser of the Year" later. It just means that the person is building the *basis* for a professional identity. If newer faculty members try to be known for success in everything, they often find that they're not recognized for success in anything.

Faculty development opportunities for newer faculty members should also be focused on developing maximum faculty engagement, a topic that will be discussed in the next chapter. If people feel as though they have become valued and respected members of the institutional community during their first five years of employment, they're likely to retain that feeling throughout the rest of their career at the institution. If they don't develop that feeling during their first five years, they're unlikely to develop it at all. And alienation often leads to attrition.

So, administrators in charge of faculty development programs should ask themselves (and, more importantly, ask new faculty members) what sorts of resources and opportunity best promote institutional loyalty. Free tickets to cultural events, lectures, athletic competition, and other community-building events for all untenured members of the faculty might be a good place to start. Newer faculty members are at a stage of their careers when they can least afford to pay admission to events. And yet, it is by attending these events that people most often feel "I belong here" at a college or university.

Supervisors can also build engagement by looking for creative ways in which to allow newer faculty members "flex time" to address whatever's going on in their lives as well as the professional demands placed upon them. In Chapter 2, the advantages of having a tenure stop-clock policy were explained. The strict rules of "up or out after six years" were created during a time when both the professor's job and social norms were different from what they are now. When these rules were created, they were intended to protect faculty members from institutions taking advantage of their labor for many years only to refuse them tenure.

In the current academic world, however, there are plenty of valid reasons why it may take longer than six years for a faculty member to develop a portfolio that would lead to promotion and either tenure or a long-term contract. The more liberal a tenure stop-clock policy is, the less likely it is that an institution will end up losing many of the faculty members it would most like to keep.

One important way for institutions to make their tenure stop-clock policies more equitable is to combine them with a plan that will adjust the faculty member's salary for income lost while the tenure clock was paused. Two faculty members at Adelphi University, Reem Khamis-Dakwar, professor of communication sciences and disorders, and Joshua Hiller, assistant professor of mathematics and computer science, note that the way most institutions' tenure stop-clock policies are written now, they end up hurting the very people they are trying to help.

The reason why these well-intentioned policies end up being ineffective (or worse) is that they disproportionately affect women, who still play a larger role in childcare than men, and members of minority groups, who frequently do not have the savings and disposable income to invest in childcare. As a result, they end up paying money for childcare out of pocket while their tenure clocks are stopped and simultaneously miss out on the salary increases that come with early promotion and any merit raises that would compound the effect of those increases.

As Khamis-Dakwar and Hiller explain the problem,

> [W]e should examine how [pausing the tenure clock and similar policies] might hurt the very faculty members they are meant to help. For example, consider a hypothetical case where a tenure-track faculty member starts at a university and receives annual raises of 3 percent with $5,000 raises upon promotion—a fairly typical compensation structure. Let's assume that the faculty member receives promotion to full professor after five years of service as an associate professor. In this case, a single one-year pause could lead to decreased earning of almost $18,000 over a 30-year career, according to our estimates. If the faculty member takes two yearlong pauses—perhaps for family leave and then separately for COVID-19—that person would lose more than $35,000 in income over the same period. . . . Academics have long decried the cruel inconsistency between healthy—and equitable—living and the tenure-track process. The

tenure process sends a clear message: life-altering events such as parenthood, divorce or a pandemic unlike any humanity has encountered in the last century shouldn't affect research output or teaching evaluations. Times of crisis can usher in revolutionary change and if we owe these faculty and the communities they serve anything, it is the reimagining and enactment of a more equitable tenure review process. Instead of pausing the tenure clock, let us really think what an equitable tenure process looks like. Part of that should be that life cannot, and should not, be put on hold for the professoriate. Life happens: babies happen, marriage happens, illness happens, unforeseen crises happen. Let us be vigilant that our solutions do not exacerbate already existing inequalities—and instead be thoughtful and helpful in our responses. (Khamis-Dakwar and Hiller, 2020)

That argument is well made. A tenure stop-clock policy is only truly equitable (and thus likely to lead to better faculty retention) if it is paired with a policy that allows a faculty member to make up this otherwise-lost income. Very few systems currently do this.

In addition, it should be remembered that the concept of "flex time" isn't limited to pausing the tenure clock; it can also apply to the faculty member's daily schedule. Certainly, college professors have long enjoyed far more flexible workdays than have employees outside of academia. But well-intentioned policies, such as a minimum number of in-person office hours to facilitate greater accessibility to students, can become obstacles for faculty members with children or who are taking care of aging parents.

Students today are quite comfortable communicating through electronic media. Many of them even prefer to use email, videoconferencing, or text messages over in-person meetings. A sensible policy that allows faculty members to meet *part* of their office-hours commitment by means of "virtual office hours" becomes yet another way in which a school says to newer faculty members, "We understand what you need at this stage in your career, and we support you enough that we are willing to provide it." (For additional ways to serve newer faculty members, see Buller, 2010, 57–66.)

WHAT MID-CAREER FACULTY MEMBERS WANT AND NEED

There is a stereotype outside higher education of the faculty member who, after receiving tenure, stops caring about preparing for classes, engaging in research, or working on committees. And, indeed, if you've worked at a college or university long enough, you may well have met someone who fits that description. But the fact is that the vast majority of mid-career faculty members continue to be productive, creative professionals.

They're devoted to their work, even though they may want to work a little differently from how they had to work as newer faculty members. In fact, in a study performed by Cindy Manjounes at Walden University, it was discovered that there is no statistically significant difference in research productivity between tenured and non-tenured faculty members (Manjounes, 2016).

The first six or seven years of a faculty position can seem like a sprint. How many articles can I publish and how quickly? How many grants can I receive in the limited time available? How can I increase my student evaluation scores until they're near the top of my program? Once that sprint is over, however, the career of a college professor becomes more like running a marathon. How do I maintain my stamina for the long haul? How do I reach those long-term goals? How can I make the transition from being so fixated with quantity (because promotion review committees, despite all the evidence indicating that doing so is not the best way to identify excellence, still tend to count things) to a more sustainable focus on quality?

For newer faculty members, the hard truths outlined above included the recommendation to concentrate on a single area of excellence, one special aspect of the professor's job that the person can become known for. The reason, as was explained, is that newer faculty members need a solid foundation upon which to build later. By the time someone has become a mid-career faculty member, that "later" has arrived. So, the question becomes, "Who do I want to be *now*?"

Retaining your best faculty thus involves helping people answer that question in a way that still involves working in your program. In many ways, mid-career faculty members have a better chance of relocating or shifting careers than do those at other stages of their professional journeys. Changing jobs as a newer faculty member typically involves a lateral move; people do it when they're dissatisfied with their current positions, colleagues, or supervisors, but they frequently receive little, if any, financial benefit from such a move. Full professors are expensive for other schools to hire. Your most distinguished professors will always be "poachable," but for the type of professor who's really very good but not a superstar, it can be difficult to obtain a job elsewhere.

Associate professors have options. If they've made a name for themselves either as a phenomenal teacher or world-class researcher at your school, they now have a stepping-stone to a lucrative career elsewhere. (Mind you, the best thing you can do for them professionally is to let them take advantage of these options. But, for the moment, the focus of this book will be on those stellar college professors that you'd do almost anything to keep.) In addition, you may be competing with other divisions of your own school for these faculty members. At mid-career certain college professors leave full-time academic appointments for administrative assignments. You could thus lose your best mid-career faculty members, not only to jobs at other schools, but to positions in the office of the dean, provost, or president.

Your goal at this point shouldn't be to "trap" these faculty members so that they stay. Neither you nor they will benefit from having someone in your program whose focus is always on "what might have been." Instead, it's important to consider what incentives you can provide to make faculty members genuinely *want* to stay. Your program recruited these professors once. Now it's time to "re-recruit" them.

Everyone's familiar with the concept of a *midlife crisis*, that period in a person's life when he or she wonders "Is this all there is?" and is tempted to seek out new opportunities and new challenges, even if the choices that are made aren't always very wise. Less familiar is the concept of the *mid-career crisis*, which similarly involves wondering "Is this all there is?" and the temptation to seek out new opportunities and new challenges, even those that are not always wise. More than one faculty member has left a promising job for work elsewhere only to discover that "the grass isn't always greener." Retaining mid-career faculty members is thus often a matter of helping people understand, as candidly and objectively as you can, how "green the grass is" here.

Many mid-career faculty members looking for "something more" begin to consider leadership positions, such as department chair, dean, or provost. And for certain faculty members, that's an excellent choice. They're already experienced, not only with how higher education works in general, but also with how your specific institution works. They may already have served on one or more major committees and perhaps even completed a term on the faculty senate or its equivalent.

Faculty members seeking administrative positions sometimes look for possibilities at other institutions, and that can cause attrition of some of your best colleagues. As always, if leaving your school is in their best interest either personally or professionally, then by all means that's the choice they should make. But sometimes people begin looking for positions at other institutions primarily because they can't see any opportunity for career progress at their own schools. If that's the case, you can help retain these highly competitive faculty members by providing local opportunities for career advancement and training resources on how to develop their leadership skills.

Local opportunities for career advancement could include informal leadership positions, such as departmental director of faculty development, college-level master teacher, or public relations officer for the division. They can also include expanded positions at the assistant or associate level with a portfolio of responsibilities in such areas as outcomes assessment, accreditation, online learning, or advising. Every institution has needs in critical areas with no one specifically assigned to address those needs. Creating an informal leadership position thus produces benefits for both the faculty member and the school. It's the classic win-win situation.

Offering training resources on leadership skill development is a highly desirable complement to the informal opportunities that you create. Many people want to lead but don't really know *how* to lead. As a result it's not uncommon for people in new academic leadership positions, no matter whether those positions are formal or informal, to be a bit too "hands on," *telling* people what to do instead of *guiding* them toward what they should do. Offering resources to attend an Academic Impressions workshop (www.academicimpressions.com), Magna Publications' Leadership in Higher Education Conference (www.magnapubs.com), or Kansas State University's Academic Chairpersons Conference (conferences.k-state.edu/academicchairpersons/) is a great place to start.

If a faculty member whom you want very much to keep does decide to take a position at another university, either as a lateral move or to try out an administrative role, you might explore the possibility of having that person take an unpaid leave of absence from your institution rather than resigning entirely. In that case, if the grass really does turn out not to be as green as he or she had hoped, it's far easier for the faculty member to return to your school.

Finally, there are other possibilities that you can offer to mid-career faculty members who may need a fresh new direction. Fulbright Fellowships allow academic professionals to work abroad for a few weeks up to a year (and sometimes even longer with an extension) for teaching, research, or both. Summer stipends provided by the National Endowment for the Humanities (NEH) support continuous full-time work on a humanities project for a period of two consecutive months. NEH Summer Seminars and Institutes provide stipends plus tuition-free one- to four-week educational programs that can serve to kick-start a stalled research agenda or bring new life to a faculty member's courses.

A good place to begin your strategy for retaining highly desirable mid-career faculty members is with a candid mentoring conversation about their current needs and career goals. Often a faculty member will tell you that he or she is thinking about leaving either for a higher salary or because "I just want something new." Those salary needs can be real—mid-career faculty members may have children in college or be supporting an elderly parent—but they can also stem from a need to be appreciated or rewarded.

If you're unable to make salary adjustments at your school, consider other ways in which you can make the faculty member feel appreciated. Review the suggestions about public and private appreciation presented in Chapter 1. Encourage the president and provost to reach out to the faculty member to show support. Look for ways, other than salary increases, to reward the person such as the one-time investments mentioned in Chapter 1.

But if the faculty member is more interested in "something new" primarily because he or she feels bored or senses that his or her career may have stalled, seeking new opportunities within your institution may be preferable to allowing that faculty member to seek new opportunities outside the institution. At least then you won't have lost 100 percent of that person's ongoing contributions to the success of your program. (For additional ways to serve mid-career faculty members, see Buller, 2010, 67–74.)

Peter Monaghan, a journalist who specializes in higher education issues, notes that outstanding mid-career faculty members are often the most difficult to retain.

> [A]ssociate professors are less satisfied than full professors and even than assistant professors, over whom the tenure broadsword still hovers. . . . Disillusionment can often begin when stapled to the back of the tenure notification is a raft of service assignments, for instance. And studies have shown that women and minority faculty members are most overloaded with service chores, and often additional teaching duties, too, and that all new associates struggle to squeeze research into their schedules. What's more, salary compression affects the associate rank most. Professors at mid-career may wonder how it is that recent hires and even junior faculty all seem better off. And regardless of how relatively "privileged" associate professors are as tenured academics, they may feel slighted and underappreciated. (Monaghan, 2017)

Monaghan's solution is to make special efforts to make sure that mid-career faculty members are content, particularly in their first three years after receiving tenure. Once most associate professors have moved beyond that three-year mark, their likelihood of remaining at the institution for the rest of their career increases significantly.

The efforts needed to make faculty members "content," to use Monaghan's word, include paying attention to the fact that many mid-career professors experience the stress of raising families at the same time that they're often caring for elderly parents and attempting to earn their next promotion. But they also include career planning services focused specifically on the questions that mid-career faculty members tend to ask about their futures. Within the time remaining before their retirement, how can they reach the goals they've now set for themselves? Achieving these goals may require some advanced training in time management and work-life balance.

In consultation with Terrence J. McDonald, former dean of the University of Michigan at Ann Arbor's College of Literature, Science, and the Arts, Monaghan also recommends being sensitive to the vocabulary used when trying to retain mid-career faculty members. The term *mentors* is regarded by some associate professors as demeaning. They're not fresh out of graduate school. They want *feedback from colleagues*, not *mentoring*. Many of them also don't want *service* obligations. They want *leadership* and *governance* opportunities.

Although those changes can seem minor, they're all part of being responsive to the needs and desires of faculty members at this important stage of their careers. It's one way of demonstrating that the institution understands them and values them as members of its community.

WHAT SENIOR FACULTY MEMBERS WANT AND NEED

Although attrition of full professors is less common than it is for those who hold the rank of assistant or associate professor, it still occurs. And when it does occur, it can be particularly problematic because of the institutional memory and level of expertise that is lost. So, how do academic leaders increase the likelihood that their best senior faculty members will remain at their colleges and universities?

If the primary question that newer faculty members ask is "How do I get promoted?" and the primary question mid-career faculty members ask is "Is this all there is?" the primary question that many senior faculty members ask is "What will my legacy be?" The legacy involved may be at the institution, to the discipline, as a person generally, or some combination of all three.

The mistake that many colleges and universities make is believing that senior faculty members don't need any type of ongoing professional development. The assumption appears to be "They've already established themselves as teachers and scholars. What would we be developing them for?" But the fact remains that each stage of a faculty member's career brings its own opportunities and challenges, and targeted programs for senior faculty members benefit the institution as much as they benefit the faculty members themselves.

Programs that guide senior faculty members to deal with the issue of their legacy can include those that help professors "pay it forward" in terms of helping others in the way that they themselves were (or wished they were) helped. Many full professors are eager to help junior faculty members succeed, but they don't always know how. They assume that the way they themselves achieved success is the way that *all* faculty members must achieve success and thus are overly prescriptive when they should encourage those whom they're helping to build a career on their own terms.

For this reason, programs like "Coaching and Mentoring for Senior Faculty Members" can help professors make a positive contribution by teaching them more effective ways to coach (i.e., instructing someone how to *do* something, such as teach a large class or write an effective grant proposal) or mentor (i.e., instructing a person how to *be* something, such as a department chair or faculty senate leader) people at the beginning or middle of their careers. These programs can explain why coaches and mentors need to listen as much as they speak and to adapt strategies to fit the individual goals of each faculty member they assist.

Other faculty development initiatives that can assist senior faculty members are those that help them develop wholly new interests or to move into new areas of scholarly inquiry. Far too many faculty members have thought, "Once I retire I'll have time to learn photography/practice mindfulness meditation/work in the garden/engage in some other hobby or activity" only to discover that it's very difficult to start a new activity without the support system they've relied on throughout their careers. Being a professor one day and a hobbyist the next can be an abrupt transition for many people. It's far easier to develop additional interests while you're still working full-time and then devote more time to those interests after retirement than to develop those interests suddenly upon retirement.

What all of this means is that faculty development programs benefit from offering courses and modules on topics that may not initially seem relevant to faculty work. Remember that the goal of faculty development is to provide resources for every aspect of what a college professor does, and some of those aspects (particularly for senior professors) include their activities off campus as well as in the laboratory or classroom.

The opportunities offered by your faculty development program can include traditional hobbies like photography or watercolor painting, wellness activities like qi gong or yoga, book clubs, and financial planning courses such as how to restructure an investment portfolio after retirement. These opportunities provide senior faculty members with an inducement to stay at your institution by offering them a chance to grow that they may not have elsewhere.

Senior faculty members also can be good ambassadors for your institution or program. They know a great deal about the institution, and so can answer questions that prospective students or donors might have. Even in these cases, however, a little advance training may be required. Full professors may know the requirements of their own programs very well but may not understand those in other academic areas. They may have a sense of the school's financial needs but not understand appropriate and effective ways of fundraising. Providing training in these areas both serves as a growth opportunity for the professor and helps avoid the dissemination of incorrect information.

Finally, colleges and universities should consider the possibility of creating new ranks. Many faculty members are promoted to the rank of full professor in their thirties or forties. That means that they have no opportunity for promotion to a higher rank for twenty years or more of their career. Promotion is one of the ways in which people in any profession are made to feel that they're making progress. The fact that higher education primarily has only three ranks (not including such positions as instructor or lecturer) can cause many senior faculty members to feel that their career has been stalled.

To avoid this problem, it can be beneficial to create new positions such as *senior professor*, *distinguished professor*, or *eminent scholar*. Some schools even refine these titles further by specifying the area in which the faculty member has excelled, such as *senior research professor*, *distinguished teaching professor*, or *eminent leadership scholar*. The goal is thus to reward continued contributions by the most accomplished members of the faculty and to give them a goal to strive for even when they've already achieved the rank of full professor. (For additional ways to serve senior faculty members, see Buller, 2010, 75–81.)

THE PROS AND CONS OF COUNTEROFFERS

Faculty members whom you'd very much like to retain may occasionally tell you that they've received an attractive offer from another institution and ask you if you'd like to match it. Making a counteroffer has both advantages and disadvantages. On the plus side, it can be the only way you can prevent one of your best faculty members from leaving, and at some institutions it's nearly the only way you can give someone a substantial pay raise outside of the regular system of merit increases and inequity adjustments. On the negative side, it can induce some faculty members to apply for jobs they have no interest in taking simply to qualify for a counteroffer.

This last problem is significant. It means that the faculty member has wasted time on submitting an application, visiting another institution, and being interviewed that could better have been devoted to research, improvements to teaching, or service activities at your own school. It means that your institution may develop a poor reputation among its peers for allowing its faculty members to waste their time and money with useless interviews. And it means that you may end up making an offer which causes salary compression or inversion you would have rather avoided.

For all of these reasons, academic leaders should try to change any institutional policy requiring a written offer before an out-of-cycle salary increase can be made to truly outstanding faculty members. Allowing significant increases to be made only as a counteroffer wastes the time of the faculty member and the institution that tried to hire the faculty member. It makes colleges and universities less efficient at the very time when most academic leaders are trying to increase the efficiency and sustainability of their programs.

Nevertheless, there are times when you do want to make a counteroffer because one of your best faculty members is being lured by another institution. When that happens, consider taking the following steps:

- Have a candid conversation with the faculty member about why he or she is considering the other offer. Is it because of salary, dissatisfaction with his or her current position, or something else? If it's because of salary, a financial counteroffer may well be effective. If it's because of job dissatisfaction, financial counteroffers don't work very well; you may need to address the cause of the dissatisfaction instead of or in addition to making a financial counteroffer. If it's for some other reason, such as relocating to be nearer to family, you may not be able to address that reason directly; the best you may be able to do is to suggest that the person take a leave of absence rather than resigning, just in case the new position doesn't work out as well as he or she had hoped.
- If you decide to make a counteroffer, consider the implications. The faculty member's new salary may cause issues of salary compression or inversion. You may be opening the door to anyone else who wants to seek a salary increase by bringing you an offer from another institution. Would you be accused of playing favorites if you don't do for someone else what you've done for this person? Can you live with that? In addition, if you make a counteroffer now, what will you do if the same faculty member brings you another offer next year or even in a few months? Will you try to make an additional counteroffer then, too? None of these questions are meant to imply that you shouldn't go ahead and try to retain the faculty member. There are times when counteroffers are the only way that academic leaders can retain their best faculty members. But you should only embark on this process with your eyes open. Counteroffers never just affect the faculty members who receive them.
- Remember that a counteroffer doesn't always have to match or exceed the original offer. Sometimes faculty members will regard almost any effort by their current institutions to accommodate them as reason enough for remaining. Relocating is expensive, after all. And the person may be farther ahead financially by remaining at his or her current institution with a smaller salary increase rather than moving somewhere else with a larger salary increase.
- Remember, too, that a counteroffer doesn't have to be made in the area of salary if that's not possible at your institution or you can't afford it. You might be able to make the faculty member's life better in other ways. Can you offer a larger office? A different schedule? A change in title or responsibilities? There may even be benefits that your institution offers that aren't available at the school that's trying to lure away your

valued faculty member. Many private institutions offer tuition remission to dependents while many public institutions don't. The savings in tuition that your school provides could well be several times more than the salary increase the faculty member is receiving, particularly if he or she will have several college-age children in the near future. As a result, think in terms of the entire package your institution is providing the faculty member, not in terms of salary alone.

BEST PRACTICES IN PROVIDING SUPPORT AT KEY POINTS IN SOMEONE'S CAREER

Some colleges and universities already have in place excellent policies on how best to support faculty members at key points in their careers. If you're interested in expanding your school's efforts in these regards, you have plenty of role models to choose from.

The University of Washington (UW) has implemented a Faculty Retention Initiative that's operated out of the provost's office. Through this initiative, UW's Office for Faculty Advancement (which also deals with such issues as searches and faculty development) works collaboratively with programs to help retain the university's best faculty members.

Although the Faculty Retention Initiative was designed to promote diversity and inclusion, UW makes it very clear that "the focus of diversity, equity, and inclusion is not on the demographic background of faculty but on the intellectual direction of their work and that work's proven or potential impact" (Faculty Retention Initiative, 2020). In other words, the initiative is not just a *minority* faculty retention plan, but a retention plan that can help the university serve a broader and more diverse community. For example, non-minority college professors whose specialties help to diversify the student body or that address the concerns of a diverse community can also be served by this program.

UW's initiative is intended to assist with the retention of tenure-track and tenured faculty through the types of one-time investments that were discussed above.

> Funds totaling $500,000 are available to contribute to the efforts of a college, school, or campus to retain talented faculty whose research, teaching, mentoring, service, and/or outreach assists the university in meeting its goals for diversity, inclusion, equity, and equal opportunity. . . . **One-time funds** may be requested for a specified number of years on a cost-sharing basis with units, colleges, schools, and/or campuses. Funds may be used for purposes including but not limited to summer salary support or supplemental research support

(including research assistance support, staff support, professional travel, supplies and equipment, publication support, etc.). **These funds cannot be used for regular salary**. (Faculty Retention Initiative, 2020; emphasis in original)

To achieve this goal, the university has developed a simple one-page form that academic leaders can submit to the provost's office, identifying the faculty member whom the program wishes to retain, the way in which the funds will be spent (as summer salary, research funds, or something else), and the period over which the funds will be allocated (UW Faculty Retention Initiative, n.d.).

The program submitting the form is also expected to offer a written case for how the faculty member enhances the unit's diversity profile and why there is a need for a retention effort (including both existing *and* potential outside offers). The removal of the need for the faculty member to submit an actual written offer from another institution reduces the likelihood that people will divert the time they could be spending on their teaching or research to applying for jobs they have no intention of accepting. UW's policy is that regular reviews and updates of salaries, benefits, job satisfaction, and workloads can help *prevent* faculty members from seeking outside offers.

One idea that academic leaders might consider, therefore, is to do a comprehensive study of where faculty development funding is available at their institutions and provide this information as a service to the faculty. Departments and colleges might have limited funds, but funding might be available through the office of the undergraduate dean, the graduate school, or the division of research. Provosts' offices sometimes offer stipends that can be used for professional development, and presidents' offices sometimes have awards that serve a similar purpose.

Faculty members can't apply for these opportunities if they don't know about them. So, good leadership may entail collecting and disseminating the information that helps the faculty even when you're unable to disseminate funds.

Columbia University is another school that offers its programs guidance on how to deal with outside offers received by its faculty members. That advice begins with observations made by researchers James L. Price, Laura L. B. Barnes, Menna O. Agago, and William T. Coombs that faculty turnover was most likely due to job dissatisfaction relating to time constraints and other commitments than salary alone (Price, 1989; and Barnes, Agago, and Coombs, 1998). It then proceeds to recommend strategies for programs to counter this dissatisfaction, such as:

- offer a lighter teaching load;

- consider an Exemption from Teaching Duties (ETD) for that faculty member (see Faculty Handbook for criteria for ETD);
- provide more flexibility with time commitments;
- match the offer monetarily or in research funds; and
- support faculty research through funding, seed monies, time, and other resources. (Office of the Provost, 2018, 15)

In and of itself, none of that advice seems particularly unusual. What makes Columbia's approach such a good role model, however, is the extent that its policy for retention goes beyond this advice to include the comprehensive system for addressing faculty concerns that was mentioned in Chapters 2 and 3. For example, the university's *Guide to Best Practices in Faculty Retention* (Office of the Provost, 2018) contains a number of checklists that programs can use to audit whether their strategies in such areas as departmental climate, program for welcoming new faculty members, faculty development, and the like meet the institution's standards.

The guide even offers specific indicators of success, much in the same way that schools offer such indicators for the assessment of student learning outcomes. These indicators include a decline in faculty attrition over time, scores on departmental morale and campus climate surveys, level of faculty awareness regarding institutional policies and standards for promotion, and the number of networking opportunities provided to faculty members each year.

If a program finds that it doesn't meet the university's indicator for success in any category, Columbia then offers a strategy for the program and directs it to the resources available for implementing that strategy. What is most impressive about this approach is that the strategies are not generic, but tailored to the needs of junior faculty, mid-career faculty, and senior faculty.

For example, if a program's internal audit suggests that its senior faculty is experiencing occupational stress, workload imbalance, limited opportunities to expand their research or obtain higher positions, or attractive job offers from other institutions, the university recommends the following approach:

- Support faculty through this transition
- Encourage faculty to pursue their intellectual interests
- Monitor their service and teaching commitments, allowing faculty to cut back on some duties
- Provide leadership training opportunities for senior faculty as a key pathway to enhancing academic governance
- Train faculty on cultural sensitivity, being an ally, and sustaining an inclusive climate
- Facilitate targeted professional training and development for faculty (Office of the Provost, 2018, 21)

The guide then directs the program to the following resources for senior faculty:

- The Provost Leadership Fellows Program [, which] aims to develop leadership skills for some of our outstanding tenured faculty
- The Columbia University Irving Medical Center (CUIMC) Summer Institute for Teaching and Learning [, which] is a one-day workshop for junior faculty or senior faculty who have taken on a new teaching role
- The CUIMC Leadership and Management Course for Faculty [, which] is a four-day program designed for faculty who currently have leadership/management responsibilities or who wish to include these in their career goals (Office of the Provost, 2018, 22)

Similar strategies and tailored resources are outlined for junior faculty, mid-career faculty, and underrepresented faculty. This highly nuanced approach is light-years ahead of the advice to "make a counteroffer and recommend some faculty development opportunities" that all too many schools rely on. By providing the right kind of support at critical points in a faculty member's career, the Columbia system for faculty retention increases the likelihood that the school's best faculty members will actually be retained.

Carnegie Mellon University is an example of an institution that has included faculty retention in its strategic plan. Among the steps the university is taking to pursue this goal are the following:

- Remain vigilant in retaining outstanding faculty, including relevant funding support and salary considerations, capitalizing on the unique attributes of the university environment in comparison to many better-resourced institutions.
- Create a formal network for mentorship to nurture and support junior faculty throughout their tenure at Carnegie Mellon.
- Tightly couple the development of professional and leadership skills with advancement opportunities for all faculty, with an intentional focus on junior faculty, women and underrepresented minorities.
- Promote engagement among faculty, across disciplines, as well as connections with administrators, staff and alumni, enhancing civility and social engagement while building strong networks of support.
- Address specific career-life issues, including enhanced access to childcare and dual-career issues, to help faculty facilitate career success in tandem with meaningful family life, address personal health and well-being, and navigate other life events.

- Further advance the current trajectory of more active engagement and collaborations between faculty and administration, including increasing opportunities for shared governance.
- Within a context of transparency, create and welcome opportunities for faculty to leverage their expertise to inform university best practices in matters operational, curricular and developmental. (Strategic Plan 2025, 2020)

Carnegie Mellon presents these strategies not merely as a budget-protection or community-building effort, but as vital elements in its efforts to diversify its community, have a positive impact on its community, direct resources toward the physical and emotional well-being of its stakeholders, and build on its core of world-renowned faculty members.

While this plan does address the need for making attractive counteroffers and generally addressing salary issues that may induce some professors to leave, not all of its initiatives are resource-intensive. Many schools already have mentoring programs for new faculty members. It's not particularly expensive to review a mentorship program that's already in place at a college or university and make sure that it's actually meeting the needs of those it was designed to serve. A well-designed mentoring program can actually improve the retention of both junior and more senior faculty members: The junior faculty members receive the advice and support they need; the mid-career and senior faculty members receive a sense of satisfaction (and sometimes a stipend) for making a positive difference in their colleagues' development.

In a similar way, it's not particularly expensive to expand faculty development programs that are probably already in place so that they include leadership development opportunities and allow "faculty to leverage their expertise to inform university best practices." In fact, doing so can actually be a cost *saving* measure since, by providing those already under contract with the chance to apply their knowledge to the improvement of the university, it reduces the need for Carnegie Mellon to hire external experts and consultants for this purpose.

Of particular importance is Carnegie Mellon's emphasis on promoting engagement and enhancing civility. An old saying in human resources circles is "People don't leave jobs. They leave bosses." In the context of higher education, this observation might be expanded to say, "Faculty members don't leave jobs. They leave unsupportive environments." Environments can seem unsupportive because they appear hostile, overly politicized, uncivil, or merely indifferent. A comprehensive plan for faculty retention thus should address not merely the needs and desires of individual faculty members, but the overall community in which they work. It should ask the question, "What would make a faculty member *want* to become more engaged with our institution at each stage of his or her career?"

One final example of an institution that serves as an excellent role model for practices intended to improve faculty retention is Cornell University. Adopting and adapting recommendations found in JoAnne Moody's *Faculty Diversity* (2014), Cornell offers its programs such advice as the following:

- Include faculty development opportunities in annual review conversations. Provide feedback on the faculty member's personal assessment of the year, as well as on his or her plans for the upcoming year. Gather ideas from the faculty member to improve his/her experience and the department and discuss any events over the course of the past year that might necessitate a tenure clock extension.
- Encourage mid-career professional development to support faculty as they work toward promotion to full professorship. Address career development early and often, so that it is not perceived as a punitive discussion when it occurs. Encourage creativity in new directions and provide mentoring or networking resources.
- Develop and maintain objective criteria for granting tenure and promotions and inform faculty of these expectations. While it is impossible to guarantee any element of the faculty reward system, the process should be openly communicated to prevent unnecessary anxiety. Although there may be no single scale against which all cases are measured, it is still useful to share as much detail as possible. Any formal descriptions should be supplemented with more informal information-sharing opportunities such as promotion and tenure workshops offered either in the department [or] by the college. . . .
- Foster a supportive environment by engaging senior faculty in discussions about their role as mentors, encouraging peer mentoring networks and engaging all faculty in discussions about governance and decision-making in the department.
- Recognize important faculty contributions in all areas including teaching, research, service, and creative activities.
- Use a variety of resources (salary adjustments, chaired professorships, reduced loads, leaves, bridge money, research support, mentors, etc.) to recruit and retain faculty. Resources decisions should be made on a case-by-case basis.
- Offer opportunities for faculty professional development, collaboration and networking within and across ranks.
- Advocate flexible and accommodating policies and practices that can improve the experience of faculty and help with retention. Know what

policies and practices are already in place at Cornell for work-life balance. . . .
- Protect junior faculty from *excessive* teaching, advising, and service assignments. Do encourage them to choose a moderate number of these activities to help acculturate them to the department and the university and begin to make connections with colleagues.
- Provide new faculty with training in time management, effective communication, teaching and grant-writing.
- Actively work to help new faculty make scholarly connections within and outside the department.
- Develop with new faculty annual and career plans. Involve mentors in the development of these plans. . . .
- Assign senior faculty the responsibility for actively mentoring newcomers. Prepare senior faculty to act as mentors and resources for new faculty. . . . (Good Practices for Retention of Faculty, n.d.)

This advice provides almost a checklist for how a college or university can begin to develop a plan for retaining faculty members by addressing their needs at specific points in their careers. If all institutions began following these guidelines, their challenges to faculty retention would not be eliminated, of course, but they would almost certainly be reduced to a more manageable level.

CONCLUSION

Obviously, not every college or university has the resources of a Columbia University, a Cornell, or a Carnegie Mellon University to devote to the challenge of retaining its faculty. So, what do you do if you don't have the funding to make attractive counteroffers or even to expand your current faculty development program?

First, go through the best practices listed above and select those that either have no cost or that can be implemented at a very small cost. These practices include:

- Taking full advantage of course releases, reassignments, or faculty development programs already in place
- Conducting an internal audit of your departmental climate, program for welcoming new faculty members, and mentoring opportunities
- Providing formal and informal recognition of those faculty members who demonstrate success in any aspect of their responsibilities

- Sitting down and talking to faculty members about their current needs, desires, and career plans
- Identifying and calculating the cost of benefits, like tuition remission for relatives, that faculty members might not receive at other institutions
- Clarifying standards and expectations for promotion, tenure, and merit increases so that faculty members understand exactly what they need to do in order to be successful in these processes

If you can demonstrate success in reducing faculty attrition with these practices, use that information to advocate for institutional investment in faculty retention.

Second, once you receive that institutional investment, begin expanding your retention program by adding one or more of the following practices:

- Establishing a fund that can be used for one-time investments that will help promote faculty retention
- Supporting faculty travel to conferences for the sake of learning and networking, not merely making presentations
- Making at least partial counteroffers (in ongoing or one-time funding) to faculty members who are being lured by other institutions
- Addressing challenges for childcare, eldercare, and dual-career couples that may be causing faculty dissatisfaction

Even though these activities do require some investments, remember one important factor as you make your case for additional funding to help retain faculty members: Searches are expensive, and salaries for incoming faculty members tend to rise more quickly than do salaries for faculty members who remain at the institution. For this reason, *it is always less expensive for a college or university to retain an existing faculty member than to hire a replacement.*

KEY POINTS IN THIS CHAPTER

- Faculty development consists of providing training, resources, and other support for all aspects of what a faculty member does. It does not consist merely of training in how to teach or conduct research better.
- Truly effective faculty development programs are not offered in a "one-size-fits-all" format. Rather, they recognize that faculty members have different needs and interests at various stages of their careers.

- For newer faculty members, time and money are usually the scarcest resources. Improving faculty retention thus includes addressing these needs.
- Newer faculty members should be encouraged to be highly selective about the service assignments they select and to develop a career plan that is both reasonable and flexible.
- Many junior faculty members can benefit from "flex time," but tenure stop-clock policies are not the only (and often not the best) way of providing this flexibility.
- Mid-career faculty members are often the biggest challenge for faculty retention efforts. They are far enough along in their progress to have established a solid record in teaching, research, and service but not as expensive as full professors for other institutions to "hire away."
- Faculty development opportunities for mid-career faculty members should include programs on leadership development.
- For faculty retention efforts, addressing the needs of faculty members during the first three years after they receive tenure is critical.
- The needs of senior faculty members are often addressed by allowing them to coach and mentor junior faculty members, thus "paying it forward" to the academic community.
- Senior faculty members should also receive development in activities they're likely to pursue after retirement.
- The traditional three ranks used for faculty members in higher education—assistant professor, associate professor, and professor—are no longer sufficient to promote faculty engagement and loyalty. They need to be supplemented by additional ranks and tracks (such as teaching or research) so that senior faculty members will feel that they are continuing to advance in their careers.
- Counteroffers are sometimes the only way to retain certain faculty members but they have significant drawbacks such as intensifying salary compression and inversion.
- A counteroffer does not always have to be in salary. One-time investments in equipment, travel, or office furnishings are often all it takes to persuade a valued faculty member to stay.
- Colleges and universities should abolish the practice of only offering out-of-cycle salary increases to those faculty members with a written offer from another institution. This practice only wastes the time of the faculty member and the other institution, and it creates a negative image for the institution that has this practice.
- A program designed to promote the retention of faculty members at various stages of their careers does not have to start from scratch. There are already excellent models in place at the University of

Washington, Columbia University, Carnegie Mellon University, and Cornell University.
- Programs that promote faculty retention should not be onerous for the academic leader or program using them. Long forms and the requirement for extensive documentation serve as a disincentive for people to take advantage of these programs.

REFERENCES

Barnes, L. L. B., Agago, M. O., & Coombs, W. T. (1998). Effects of job-related stress on faculty intention to leave academia. *Research in Higher Education.* 39(4), 457–469.

Buller, J. L. (2010). *The essential college professor: A practical guide to an academic career.* San Francisco, CA: Jossey-Bass.

Faculty Retention Initiative: University of Washington. (2020). https://www.washington.edu/provost/initiatives/faculty-retention-initiative/.

Good Practices for Retention of Faculty: Cornell University. (n.d.). https://cpb-us-e1.wpmucdn.com/blogs.cornell.edu/dist/8/6767/files/2017/09/Good-practices-for-retention-of-faculty-23f7bdr.pdf.

Khamis-Dakwar, R., & Hiller, J. (2020). The problems with pausing the tenure clock. *Inside Higher Ed.* https://www.insidehighered.com/advice/2020/07/07/response-pandemic-better-alternatives-pausing-tenure-clock-should-be-considered.

Manjounes, C. (2016). *How tenure in higher education relates to faculty productivity and retention.* https://scholarworks.waldenu.edu/cgi/viewcontent.cgi?article=3661&context=dissertations.

Monaghan, P. (2017). Helping professors overcome mid-career malaise. *The Chronicle of Higher Education.* https://www.chronicle.com/article/Helping-Professors-Overcome/240009.

Moody, J. (2004). *Faculty diversity: Problems and solutions.* New York, NY: Routledge.

Office of the Provost: Columbia University. (2018). *Guide to best practices in faculty retention.* https://provost.columbia.edu/sites/default/files/content/Faculty%20Diversity%20and%20Inclusion/BestPracticesFacultyRetention.pdf.

Price, J. L. (1989). The impact of turnover on the organization. *Work and Occupations.* 16(4), 461–473.

Strategic Plan 2025: Carnegie Mellon University. (2020). *Recruiting and retaining world-class faculty.* https://www.cmu.edu/strategic-plan/strategic-recommendations/recruiting-and-retaining-faculty.html.

UW Faculty Retention Initiative: Support Request Form. (n.d.). https://s3-us-west-2.amazonaws.com/uw-s3-cdn/wp-content/uploads/sites/11/2017/07/23170402/Retention-Form.pdf.

What Do Faculty Do?: American Association of University Professors. (n.d.). https://www.aaup.org/issues/faculty-work-workload/what-do-faculty-do.

RESOURCES

Baker, V. L., Lunsford, L. G., Neisler, G., Pifer, M. J., & Terosky, A. L. P. (2019). *Success after tenure: Supporting mid-career faculty.* Sterling, VA: Stylus.

Bensimon, E. M., Ward, K., & Sanders, K. (2000). *The department chair's role in developing new faculty into teachers and scholars.* Bolton, MA: Anker.

Boice, R. (1990). *Professors as writers: A self-help guide to productive writing.* Stillwater, OK: New Forum.

Boice, R. (2009). *Advice for new faculty members: Nihil* nimus. Boston, MA: Allyn & Bacon.

Lucas, C. J., & Murry, J. W. (2011). *New faculty: A practical guide for academic beginners.* New York, NY: Palgrave Macmillan.

Pettit, E. (2020). As professors scramble to adjust to the coronavirus crisis, the tenure clock still ticks. *The Chronicle of Higher Education.* https://www.chronicle.com/article/As-Professors-Scramble-to/248289.

Provitera-MacGlynn, A. (2001). *Successful beginnings for college teaching: Engaging your students from the first day.* Madison, WI: Atwood.

Roche, M. W. (2018). *Realizing the distinctive university: Vision and values, strategy and culture.* Notre Dame, IN: University of Notre Dame Press.

Welch, A. G., Bolin, J. H., & Reardon, D. (2019). *Mid-career faculty: Trends, barriers, and possibilities.* Boston, MA: Brill/Sense.

Chapter 5

Promoting Faculty Engagement

The expression *faculty engagement* has appeared many times throughout earlier chapters as a key factor in faculty retention. But what exactly *is* faculty engagement? Certainly a great deal of attention has been paid to *student* engagement in higher education. There are even centers for student engagement on many campuses and several widely used inventories, such as the National Survey of Student Engagement (nsse.indiana.edu) and the Faculty Survey of Student Engagement (fsse.indiana.edu) that have been developed.

These inventories measure practices that most faculty members would agree distinguish truly engaged students from those who are merely going through the motions. They ask about the frequency at which students studied or engaged in discussions about their courses even when there were other things to do, the number and length of the research papers they wrote, their ability to move forward after making mistakes, and similar matters. But what would it mean for a faculty member to be similarly engaged in his or her work?

Most administrators probably assume that productivity is a good (albeit indirect) measure of faculty engagement. But faculty members can still be effective teachers and prolific researchers even when they feel indifferent about or even hostile to the institutions where they work. And if those two factors become combined—truly superb teachers and scholars who have little or no attachment to their college or university—you increase the likelihood that a faculty member you'd desperately like to keep may be lured away by another institution, even if its job offer isn't particularly attractive.

The simple truth is that engaged faculty members stay at a school unless pulled away due to unforeseen personal reasons; disengaged faculty members often leave at the first opportunity. And even when disengaged faculty members *do* stay, their contributions to the success of the institution often diminish over time. So, what exactly works to promote faculty engagement?

A BRIEF HISTORY OF FACULTY ENGAGEMENT

In order to answer this question, it's helpful to understand where the whole idea of faculty engagement comes from. It's a concept that first arose in the corporate world, specifically within the domain of human resources. The figure who is regarded as the pioneer of employee engagement is William Kahn, a professor of management and organizations at Boston University. In a 1990 article, Kahn applied concepts arising from *social identity theory*—the idea that people derive a sense of who they are from the groups they belong to—to the performance of employees in a work setting (Kahn, 1990).

Kahn concluded that three psychological conditions—meaningfulness, safety, and availability—correlated strongly with employee engagement and probably had a causal relationship with it. Meaningfulness, as its name implies, involves the degree to which employees find that their work produces significant benefits for themselves, their organizations, and society as a whole. Safety involves not physical security but the sense of comfort that employees have about being themselves at work and applying who they are to their assignments without fear of negative consequences. Availability involves the degree to which employees feel mentally and physically capable of applying themselves completely to each individual task at each individual moment.

Engaged employees, therefore, *identify* with their work. When asked who they are, they say things like, "I'm a welder at Highly Engaged Industries over on Commitment Street." Unengaged employees, on the other hand, *perform* their work (and sometimes not very well). When asked who they are, unengaged employees say things like, "Oh, I'm a veteran and a member of Unaffiliated Church, and I also do welding at the Unengaged Corporation down on Passive-Aggression Street."

Employee engagement can often reflect the amount of discretionary effort people put into their jobs. But there are also several important things that employee engagement is *not*:

- Employee engagement is not static. It can ebb and flow over time. You can't simply pigeonhole people as either engaged or unengaged, assuming that this distinction is an essential part of their characters. Even the most highly engaged employees can become quickly unengaged if circumstances change. And unengaged employees can become engaged again, although much more slowly, if circumstances change.
- Employee engagement is not the same thing as employee satisfaction. An employee may be satisfied because he or she is never challenged and has fallen into a comfortable rut. Employee satisfaction has little

relationship to employee productivity. But an engaged employee is almost always a productive employee, and the work that he or she does is likely to be of very high quality.
- Employee engagement is not a technique or strategy that managers can use to get their employees to work harder. People tend to see through strategies rather quickly. A ploy used to manipulate them may work in the short term, but it will ultimately be unsuccessful. Employee engagement, on the other hand, arises out of a supervisor's interpersonal style and philosophy. Frequently, too, it is a product of the company's culture and values.

In 1999, Marcus Buckingham and Curt Coffman of the Gallup Organization published *First, Break All the Rules*, which summarized the findings of two major studies: a survey of more than a million employees in various types of companies about their workplace needs and a longitudinal study of the practices that distinguish successful from unsuccessful managers. What Buckingham and Coffman found was that the best managers focus on building the strengths of their employees, not on fixing their weaknesses, and make employee engagement a priority.

Through its authors' research, *First, Break All the Rules* provided clear evidence, perhaps for the first time, that employees leave their immediate managers, not the companies they work for. The book also introduced the set of twelve questions that became known as the Q12, the Gallup Organization's employee engagement survey. This survey contains the now famous Question 10—"I have a best friend at work."—which serves as a proxy for determining whether someone regards the workplace merely as somewhere to earn a paycheck or sees it as a community where personal loyalties and engagement are possible.

Other major works on employee engagement soon followed. In 2001, Christina Maslach, Wilmar Schaufeli, and Michael Leiter published a study in the *Annual Review of Psychology* that presented employee engagement as an effective deterrent to burnout (Maslach, Schaufeli, and Leiter, 2001). A year later, James Harter, Frank Schmidt, and Theodore Hayes published a meta-analysis of studies exploring the relationship among employee engagement, employee satisfaction, and productivity (Harter, Schmidt, and Hayes, 2002). And in 2008, Julie Gebauer and Don Lowman published *Closing the Engagement Gap*, with its five-step plan on how to improve employee engagement and reduce attrition: Know them, grow them, inspire them, involve them, and reward them, the *them* in each case being the employees.

The migration of these ideas from the corporate to the academic world followed a bit more slowly, with faculty engagement only occasionally adopted as a topic for articles, conference presentations, and doctoral dissertations.

(See, for example, Nakamura and Csikszentmihalyi, 2005; Livingston, 2011; and Raina and Khatri, 2015.) The reasons why so much attention is paid to employee engagement while relatively little is paid to faculty engagement are significant, and they reveal one of the challenges academic leaders face with regard to faculty retention.

The concept of employee engagement largely developed in the world of human resources, and faculty members sometimes bristle when they're referred to as "employees." They understand, of course, that, as people who are paid in return for their labor, they certainly fall into the category of being employees. But they see their work as distinctly different from that of an employee in the retail or corporate world.

For one thing, faculty members prize their academic freedom. Within their spheres of expertise, they're given a great deal of leeway in determining what to teach, how to teach it, and even (in many situations) when to teach it. They don't have to punch a time clock to verify that they're working when they're supposed to be working, and although they may be required to put in a certain number of office hours each week, they usually are able to determine independently when those hours are scheduled.

Faculty members thus see themselves as far more like free agents or independent contractors than typical employees. So, concepts that derive in the environment of typical manager-employee relationships are often met with suspicion by faculty members. They may therefore regard expressions like *employee engagement* as efforts to manipulate them or to reduce their status to that of mere "paid help" rather than attempts to benefit both themselves and the institution.

Complicating this situation is the fact that the very idea of an office of human resources sometimes seems alien to the world in which faculty members work. At many colleges and universities, *staff members* are hired and evaluated by the office of human resources; *faculty members* are hired and evaluated by the office of the provost or its representatives, such as a dean or department chair. To the extent that many faculty members have any relationship at all with the office of human resources, it is only to complete routine paperwork and learn about benefits programs. It's rarely, if ever, related to what faculty members view as their core mission: teaching, research, and service.

At other institutions, typically private colleges and universities, the office of human resources is viewed quite differently. There the office holds a great deal of power, determining which contracts will be renewed and which administrative positions will be continued. At these schools, the office of human resources isn't viewed as something that serves the interests of the faculty; it's viewed as something that controls the fate of faculty. The author has even experienced one university where faculty members and deans regularly spoke the words *human resources* in hushed tones, as though it were an entity to be feared and, if possible, avoided.

The result is that many faculty members don't regard any initiative arising from the division of human resources as likely to be beneficial. Professionals in human resources are either dismissed as irrelevant (or at best tangential) to their work or feared as adversaries, a type of academic Big Brother. Neither of these scenarios is likely to make the faculty eager to embrace any initiative associated with that office.

As though these factors weren't bad enough for widespread acceptance of ideas like faculty engagement, there's yet another hurdle that makes the challenge even more difficult. In a study of 522 faculty members at ten four-year colleges and universities, Jennifer Livingston discovered that when faculty members are engaged in their work they're usually not engaged in all aspects of it equally. Some may be highly engaged as teachers but less committed to their activities in research, while others may be highly devoted researchers with less attachment to their roles as teachers. Faculty members often see their roles in teaching, research, and service not as highly integrated components of the same activity but as complementary or even unconnected tasks. For this reason, Livingston suggests that

> when a faculty member is engaged in one or more of these roles, he or she will enjoy it, view it as his or her calling, feel energized by it, give attention to it, and feel confident in it. Identifying these areas of engagement and encouraging growth in them is an appropriate faculty development initiative and a starting point for restructuring faculty workloads and evaluation systems. (Livingston, 2011, 120)

She thus makes five recommendations with regard to overcoming the obstacles inherent in any attempt to promote faculty engagement:

- *If a college or university truly wishes to increase faculty engagement, it will reduce faculty workload.* As the role of the faculty has changed, college professors are increasingly asked to engage in student recruitment, fundraising, community relations, and other activities that, while expected, are not rewarded or even addressed in most faculty evaluation systems. These added responsibilities fragment the faculty role even further and may intensify a person's sense that he or she is highly engaged in teaching (or research or service) but not to the institution or the profession as a whole. By reducing or eliminating many of these added responsibilities, faculty engagement is likely to increase.
- *Workloads and evaluation criteria should be restructured.* For those activities that can't be removed from a faculty member's responsibility

for any reason, the evaluation system should be revised to recognize these contributions. Instead of a model in which every faculty member is expected to do everything, "unbundling" of responsibilities would allow faculty members to devote their energy where their talents and passion lie. Livingston recommends the introduction of *creativity contracts* that allow self-defined goals to be set over several years. Evaluation could then be conducted on the degree to which those goals are attained.

- *Shared values should be emphasized through areas of expertise.* One aspect of faculty retention that isn't commonly addressed is the extent to which faculty members don't change over the course of their careers; the institutions do. As the mission of higher education evolves, some faculty members feel "This isn't the same institution it was when it hired me." As a result, they either become disengaged or increasingly focus inwardly on their own teaching and research rather than on shared values. There is a need for each level of the school, from the department to the institution as a whole, to discuss "big-picture" issues such as the role that level plays in improving society and making the world a better place. By reminding faculty members repeatedly of how their individual specialties and interests contribute to the ongoing work of higher education, the gap between "what I do" and "what the institution does" can be narrowed.

- *Include discussions of faculty expectations at all levels of faculty development.* Newer faculty members sometimes become disengaged because the role of a faculty member isn't what they thought it would be. Mid-career and senior faculty members sometimes become disengaged because the ways in which they're expected to teach, conduct research, and contribute to service change over time. An institution can't expect a senior faculty member to become proficient in classroom technology if it isn't made clear that incorporating the latest technology into one's teaching is an expectation of the job. Livingston suggests

> that a faculty development model that could best promote comprehensive development include a centralized faculty development unit consisting of professionals with expertise in teaching and learning theories, research design, program evaluation, and organizational change. When these professional faculty developers are supplemented by individual faculty members from a variety of disciplines with content expertise and interest in faculty development, a widespread initiative consisting of reflective practice can ensue to fully develop faculty members' skills and knowledge related to their role as an educator. (Livingston, 2011, 130)

- *Institutions should foster communication and the total development of the faculty member.* If an institution is going to base its success on the attainment of student outcomes, then faculty members should be trained in, evaluated on, and recognized for their contributions to these outcomes. Outdated policies mean that many institutions still communicate the message that what they value most in faculty are the number of their publications, the size of their grants, and the level of their student course evaluations. Accreditation standards have advanced from input-based to outcome-based approaches. Why haven't faculty criteria and policies? If an institution is going to be judged on how much its students learn, then so should faculty members. If an institution is going to be commended for the extent of its community engagement, then so should faculty members. Improved communication should make it clear to faculty members that what is expected of them is the quality of the result, not how much effort or enthusiasm goes into producing that result. In a similar way, faculty development programs should be revised to include a focus on everything a faculty member does, not simply classroom instruction or grant writing, as is still the case at many institutions (Livingston, 2011, 130).

FROM EMPLOYEE ENGAGEMENT TO FACULTY ENGAGEMENT

As Jennifer Livingston's research makes clear, a great deal of work still needs to be done if employee engagement is to find a true home in the academic world as faculty engagement. How can institutions most effectively "transplant" this concept to their own environments?

In order to answer these questions, it's important to begin by remembering that the organizational culture of higher education is very different from that of the corporate and retail worlds. Despite the pleas of many legislatures for colleges and universities to be "run more like a business," the fact remains that a school simply isn't a business. Rather than having as its primary goal the creation of profit and shareholder value, an institution of higher education defines its ultimate mission as the creation and dissemination of knowledge.

> "Yes," a critic might reply, "but that's just like saying that the ultimate mission of Apple is to create and disseminate the best electronic devices it can or the ultimate mission of Nike is to create and disseminate a superior line of running shoes. Knowledge is merely the *product* of higher education. Its ultimate goal still has to be raising enough money to pay the bills and, if possible, invest in future growth. So, a college or university is still more like a business than you

imagine: It should be run in such a way as to maximize profit and the efficient use of resources."

Certainly, no academic leader would argue that "the efficient use of resources" is irrelevant to the proper management of a college or university. In order to survive, an institution has to have enough income to pay the bills. And many of the strategies for retaining faculty members mentioned in this book require money. So, why do academics continue to claim that their schools aren't businesses and shouldn't be run like businesses? And how does this distinction relate to the topic of engagement?

While there have been many attempts to adopt different and more effective organizational structures in the corporate world (see, for example, Schein and Schein, 2017; and Cameron and Quinn, 2011), it's nevertheless still true that most businesses are *hierarchical* in decision-making and *stratified* in employee classification. They're hierarchical because supervisors generally assign tasks to those they supervise, often with instructions not only about what to do but also how to do it. And they're stratified because there's a clear distinction between management and labor.

Superficially colleges and universities *seem* hierarchical and stratified as well. Their organizational charts adopt the typical shape of the social pyramid, and faculty unions make a very clear distinction between management and labor. Even where unions don't exist, everyone at the institution tends to understand who serves as management and who serves as labor.

It's only when you probe beyond this superficial level that the distinctions between a university and a corporation become apparent. At least on the academic side of the institution, relatively few decisions are made hierarchically. Presidents don't tell provosts what the content and methodology for courses should be, provosts don't tell deans, and deans don't tell chairs. Those decisions are made collaboratively by the faculty in their departments and committees. That decision-making process is more democratic than hierarchical. It's true that upper levels of the administration may be required to *approve* curricular decisions by the faculty, but they don't *originate* curricular content for the faculty. That's an important distinction.

Similarly, the categories of management and labor are far more fluid in higher education than in the corporate world. Department chairs return to the faculty all the time. At some institutions, the position of chair is rotated with each faculty member taking his or her turn. It's not unheard of for a person to be a faculty member, then the chair, then a faculty member, and then the chair again at some later date. Even deans have been known to return to the faculty, perhaps accepting another administrative assignment later and perhaps not. In any case, the person who is your colleague today could well be your supervisor tomorrow, and vice versa.

This fluidity of positions within a culture that often makes decisions in a non-hierarchical manner means that the relationship between faculty members and administrators in higher education is different from that between employees and managers in business. Moreover, a manager may well know how to do an employee's job even better than the employee does, but a dean or department chair is supervising a group of people who are experts in their own fields and who often have understanding of their disciplines that the chair or dean can't possibly have. "Leadership" in this environment has to be different from the traditional view of leaders leading followers. So does engagement. The way in which academic leaders engage faculty members requires a different set of strategies from those commonly recommended in discussions of employee engagement. (For more on the distinctive organizational culture of higher education, see Buller and Reeves, 2018, 33–37; and Buller, 2015, 12–18.)

STRATEGIES FOR FACULTY ENGAGEMENT

Because faculty members work (or at least *expect* to work) in an environment that's more collegial than hierarchical, the strategies used to promote faculty engagement need to be more collegial than hierarchical. Traditional methods of employee engagement, particularly when run by offices of human resources, strike many faculty members as patriarchal. They can sometimes convey the tone that "we're here to look after you since we know you can't always look after yourself," and that tone is unlikely to be well received in faculty circles.

Traditional approaches to employee engagement—"icebreakers" before meetings, team-building exercises at retreats, overt attempts to build institutional loyalty such as company T-shirts and group slogans—are frequently counterproductive when transferred to a college or university. Faculty members see through these techniques as attempts to get them to remain at the school and work harder, to "capture discretionary effort," in the phrase commonly used when employee engagement is discussed. There's even a leadership approach known as the Discretionary Effort Model (see, for example, Piyachat, Chanongkorn, and Panisa, 2014; and Palmer and Gignac, 2012), an expression that smacks of "branding" and that many faculty members might regard as manipulative.

In order for faculty engagement efforts to be effective, they must be collegial, focused on professional development, and voluntary. Efforts that appear to be driven top-down, focused on the needs of the institution rather than the individual, and mandated or lacking in options will probably fail. "Singing the company song" may work with some employees—and there are even some faculty members who might enjoy bonding exercises of this type—but they more often seem like invasive species when transplanted into the academic world.

Nevertheless, faculty attrition often stems from faculty disengagement, and faculty disengagement often stems from low faculty morale. So, how can academic leaders work to improve morale? The first and most important step they can take is to ask faculty members one-on-one what their current level of morale is. Faculty morale is often low because no one seems to make it a priority. Simply by asking about it, academic leaders can cause it to improve. And if they do discover that morale is low (not an uncommon phenomenon) and ask for the reasons, they're likely to come away from this conversation with a clear strategy about how to solve the problem.

The next step academic leaders can take is to provide people with options for professional development. The key word in the last sentence is *options*. Not every professional development opportunity appeals to everyone. Some will want to learn new methodologies of teaching. Others may want to improve their grant writing or increase the acceptance rate for their publications. Still others will value leadership development. By making it clear that these opportunities are available—without cost to the faculty member and recognized as important by the administration—professors will select those that are appropriate to their career trajectory. And at least some of them will be grateful for the opportunity.

The third step is to lead with transparency. Most academic leaders *believe* they're candid and transparent leaders, but the impression of the faculty may be starkly different. Candid academic leaders are those who:

- Speak kindly of others even when those people aren't around.
- Let those in their area know what their core values and priorities are and why they regard them as important.
- Make decisions based on those core values and priorities rather than disregarding them when it's convenient to do so.
- Take responsibility and make genuine apologies when they do something wrong.

The significance of the last point above is often overlooked. Many academic leaders believe that they maintain their authority by giving the appearance that they themselves did or wanted to do the right thing but circumstances, the actions of others, or the decision of a supervisor made doing so impossible. If they apologize at all, they offer non-apology apologies ("Mistakes were made."), conditional apologies ("If I did anything wrong, I'm truly sorry."), or projection apologies ("If my decision upset you, then I apologize.")

A genuine apology is one where the leader takes personal responsibility for doing something wrong, does so in a timely manner (i.e., as soon as the error is realized not only when the leader is caught), and commits never to do the same thing again. Very few faculty members expect administrators never to make mistakes. It's how the mistakes are handled that builds faculty engagement, not the complete absence of mistakes. Chip and Dan Heath, whose book *The Power of Moments* (2017) was mentioned in Chapter 3, note that loyalty often *grows* after a genuine apology. It's not that the previous level of trust is merely restored; it can actually deepen (Heath and Heath, 2017, 29).

Faculty members are most engaged when they see a clear connection between their personal goals and the goals of the institution or program. Discussion of mission, vision, and values shouldn't be about the development of bland mission statements that please everyone but excite no one. Academic leaders who talk individually with faculty members about the faculty member's individual goals and aspirations and then relate those goals and aspirations to what the institution or program stands for help create an environment where people become engaged in their work and thus want to remain.

At times the matter of mission, vision, and values goes beyond the institution itself. Some departments adopt causes like promoting literacy, eliminating particular diseases, or advancing social justice that may only be tangentially related, if at all, to the work of the program. But by being a cause that the vast majority of the people in that program care about, it serves as a source of unity for the program and builds loyalty. It enables members of the program to feel that the unit is making a positive difference in the world, not simply providing them with a paycheck.

In this way, faculty engagement most often occurs as a result of a change in culture. Outside of the academic world, employee engagement may well be possible when leaders act in an authoritarian manner; hierarchies can tolerate—they sometimes even thrive—in that environment. But in the academic world, other leadership styles, such as positive leadership, servant leadership, and consensus-based leadership, are most likely to increase engagement and decrease attrition.

CONCLUSION

The connection should have been obvious. Leaders in higher education have known for a long time that student engagement results in improved student performance and increased student retention. So, why has it taken so long for administrators to realize that faculty engagement will result in improved faculty performance and increased faculty retention? Just as the lessons of the

First Year Experience can be transferred from the student realm to the faculty realm, so can the lessons of engagement.

People don't leave positions when they feel their work in those positions is interesting and important. When you're making a positive difference in the world, you want to continue making that difference. Faculty retention must begin, therefore, with changing the way in which faculty orientation, onboarding, and development are done, but it won't reach the levels that academic leaders hope to see until it also includes serious efforts to increase faculty engagement.

KEY POINTS IN THIS CHAPTER

- As a concept, faculty engagement originated in the domains of human resources and management as *employee* engagement.
- Since faculty members often don't regard themselves as "mere employees," some of the approaches discussed in books and articles about employee engagement are not effective in the academic world.
- Faculty members also often have a complex (at times distrustful) attitude toward offices of human resources. As a result, the association of employee engagement with the field of human resources often gives it a poor reputation in academic circles.
- Faculty engagement can, therefore, *adapt* some of the strategies used for employee engagement, but those strategies must reflect the distinctive organizational culture of higher education.
- Faculty engagement isn't the same thing as satisfaction or productivity. Disengaged employees *can* be satisfied, productive, or both. Nevertheless, engaged faculty members are *likely* to have increased levels of satisfaction, productivity, and retention.
- The increased levels of workload found at many colleges and universities are a severe impediment to faculty engagement.
- In order for faculty engagement practices to be successful, they must be collegial, oriented toward each faculty member's professional development, and voluntary.
- Academic leaders who wish to improve faculty engagement will do three things: They will speak individually with faculty members about their current levels of morale and engagement, they will provide faculty members with options for the activities designed to improve faculty engagement, and they will lead with transparency.
- At many institutions, faculty engagement must occur through a culture change; it can't be improved by individual academic leaders acting alone.

REFERENCES

Buckingham, M., & Coffman, C. (1999). *First, break all the rules: What the world's greatest managers do differently*. New York, NY: Simon & Schuster.

Buller, J. L. (2015). *Change leadership in higher education: A practical guide to academic transformation*. San Francisco, CA: Jossey-Bass.

Buller, J. L., & Reeves, D. M. (2018). *The five cultures of academic development*. Washington, DC: CASE.

Cameron, K. S., & Quinn, R. E. (2011). *Diagnosing and changing organizational culture based on the competing values framework*. San Francisco, CA: Jossey-Bass.

Gebauer, J., & Lowman, D., with Gordon, J. (2008). *Closing the engagement gap: How great companies unlock employee potential for superior results*. New York, NY: Portfolio.

Harter, J. K., Schmidt, F. L., & Hayes, T. L. (2002). Business-unit-level relationship between employee satisfaction, employee engagement, and business outcomes: A meta-analysis. *Journal of Applied Psychology. 87*(2), 268–279.

Heath, C., & Heath, D. (2017). *The power of moments: Why certain experiences have extraordinary impact*. New York, NY: Simon & Schuster.

Kahn, W. (1990). Psychological conditions of personal engagement and disengagement at work. *Academy of Management Journal. 33*(4), 692–724.

Livingston, J. (2011). *Defining and measuring faculty engagement: Validation of the faculty engagement survey*. Doctoral dissertation at Azusa Pacific University. https://pqdtopen.proquest.com/pubnum/3467979.html.

Maslach, C., Schaufeli, W., & Leiter, M. P. (2001). Job burnout. *Annual Review of Psychology. 52*, 397–422.

Nakamura, J., & Csikszentmihalyi, M. (2005). Engagement in a profession: The case of undergraduate teaching. *Daedalus. 134*(3), 60–67.

Palmer, B. R., & Gignac, G. (2012). The impact of emotionally intelligent leadership on talent retention, discretionary effort and employment brand. *Industrial and Commercial Training. 44*(1), 9–18.

Piyachat, B., Chanongkorn, K., & Panisa, M. (2014). The mediate effect of employee engagement on the relationship between perceived employer branding and discretionary effort. *DLSU Business and Economics Review. 24*(1), 59–72.

Raina, K., & Khatri, P. (2015). Faculty engagement in higher education: Prospects and areas of research. *On the Horizon. 23*(4), 285–308.

Schein, E. H., & Schein, P. (2017). *Organizational culture and leadership* (5th ed.). Hoboken, NJ: Wiley.

RESOURCES

Kellerman, B. (2006). When should a leader apologize and when not? *Harvard Business Review. 84*(4), 72–81.

Tavris, C. (2020). *Mistakes were made (but not by me): Why we justify foolish beliefs, bad decisions, and hurtful acts* (3rd ed.). New York, NY: Houghton Mifflin Harcourt Trade & Reference.

Chapter 6

Part-Time Faculty, Adjuncts, and Full-Time Temps

One very important faculty constituency that is too often overlooked in discussion of retention consists of *contingent faculty members*, a category of instructors that includes part-time employees, adjuncts, and full-time temporary faculty members. That oversight is serious because it's this very constituency that colleges and universities are increasingly relying on to fulfill their missions. The American Association of University Professors (AAUP) has concluded that more than half of faculty positions today are part-time and that time-limited positions are increasingly replacing tenure-track appointments (Background Facts on Contingent Faculty Positions, n.d.).

In addition, the AAUP notes that the term *part-time faculty member* is actually a misnomer, since many of these faculty members teach as many courses as those on full-time contracts. General education courses, introductory courses in the major, and courses at community colleges and for-profit institutions have an even higher percentage of contingent faculty members than other types of courses. And while some institutions convert tenure-track lines to contingent positions for budgetary reasons, they often don't convert those positions back again when economic conditions improve. (See Background Facts on Contingent Faculty Positions, n.d.)

The US Department of Education did report, however, that the percentage of faculty members in part-time positions decreased after about 2015, but even that news isn't altogether good. The primary reason for this decline appears to be the closing of many for-profit institutions in light of growing skepticism about the value of their degrees. In other words, there has been an overall decrease in the number of faculty jobs generally, with a disproportionate amount of that decrease occurring in a segment that happened to rely primarily on contingent faculty. (See Lederman, 2019.)

Even within this shrinking faculty workforce, however, there are many reasons besides cost that lead colleges and universities to rely on contingent faculty members. Without tenure or long-term contracts, contingent faculty members allow institutions to respond more quickly to rising and falling enrollment demands. Since expectations for research and service are either low or non-existent for contingent faculty members, they can devote their full attention to excellence in instruction. And so, part-time and temporary full-time faculty members make an important contribution to a school's educational mission. They are often among the very faculty members an institution is most eager to retain.

THE DOUBLE BIND

Nevertheless, trying to retain their best part-time and temporary full-time faculty members can place academic leaders in a double bind. They can either treat them like a wholly separate group of faculty (which runs the risk of complaints that they are being given no voice in the program even though they contribute far more to its success than they receive in compensation) or treat them like everyone else (which runs the risk of complaints that they are being asked to devote hours to attending meetings, serving on committees, and engaging in professional development for which they're not compensated and which they can't afford due to their other personal and professional commitments).

This double bind arises because deans and department chairs sometimes try to address what they *believe* the needs and desires of contingent faculty members are without *asking* contingent faculty members about their needs and desires. The truth is that part-time and full-time temporary faculty members span a fairly wide spectrum. Some of them do indeed want to be treated just like any other faculty member, voting on issues related to the discipline, serving on committees, and being given opportunities for professional development. Others simply don't have the time or inclination to do so. They may be juggling several other adjunct positions, childcare or eldercare obligations, and other responsibilities that make time-consuming commitments impractical. These contingent faculty members would prefer merely to teach their courses, hold their office hours, and go home.

Misjudging the needs and desires of contingent faculty members can lead to the attrition of some excellent instructors. For this reason, retention of part-time and full-time temporary faculty members begins with the following.

- *Give contingency faculty members choices*. Ask them the degree to which they wish to be active in the affairs of the department and institution. Understand that the answers you receive may be different for

different people and even different for the same person at different times. Provide options and allow those options to be changed later.
- *Give contingency faculty members flexibility.* Because of their other commitments, they may not be able to attend meetings when they're scheduled or to be available to the extent of those faculty members who are on extended full-time contracts. Allow contingency faculty members to provide insights and to comment on proposals asynchronously through listservs, memos, REPLY ALL email chains, and so on.
- *Give contingency faculty members a path forward where one is possible.* It's not always feasible to convert part-time positions into full-time positions or temporary positions into long-term positions, but when it *is* feasible, use these opportunities to reward people who have already demonstrated their value to the program. Contingent faculty members sometimes get pigeonholed as "only an adjunct" or "only a temporary instructor," even though many of them have credentials equal to or better than those of other professors in the program. Remind the members of search committees that they shouldn't overlook contingent faculty members "because they're going to continue to work here anyway." Understand that their research productivity to date may not look the same as that of applicants who have held postdocs and tenure-track positions elsewhere. Contingent faculty members often did not have the same access to research support that other applicants may have had, even though they would have excelled at research if they'd been given the opportunity. When reviewing the records of contingent faculty members, therefore, an applicant's *potential* may at times have to be given additional emphasis.
- *Give contingent faculty members the power to say no.* Since their contracts can be non-renewed at any time, many contingent faculty members feel that they can't afford to say no when asked to perform uncompensated labor under the guise of "being a full member of the team." They may not feel comfortable speaking up about situations in which they feel taken advantage of. For this reason, the first time you get any inkling that contingent faculty members have been unhappy may be when they tell you they're leaving or simply don't accept new appointments when they're offered. Go out of your way to let contingent faculty members know that they have a voice and you respect it. Empower them to be their own advocates rather than suffering in silence.
- *Give contingency faculty members comparable pay for comparable work.* The salary discrepancy between adjunct and tenure-track faculty members can be huge. The cost per class or per student credit hour of instruction for a part-time faculty member is usually a fraction of what institutions pay to faculty members who are tenured, on tenure track, or

given long-term contracts. And that disparity increases when "permanent" faculty members receive benefits like healthcare and retirement funding that adjunct faculty members don't receive. "But that's exactly why I often have to hire contingent faculty members," an administrator might object. "My budget simply can't afford additional tenure-track lines, and I'm dealing with high student demand for courses. Besides, you have to remember that my tenure-line faculty members have research and service obligations that adjuncts don't have." All these statements may be true, but while they may explain *some* disparity in the salaries paid in higher education, they don't explain *all* the disparity. Too many adjunct faculty members have to teach courses at multiple institutions simply to make ends meet. They don't need to be paid proportionally the *same* salaries as full-time faculty members are paid, particularly if they are indeed not assigned duties outside the classroom. But they should be paid sufficiently and comparably. The pathway to building loyalty among your best contingent faculty members begins with their salaries. If your budget or institutional policies won't allow the payment of reasonable wages, then you can at least become an advocate for the changes that would make these salaries possible.

ORIENTATION AND ONBOARDING FOR CONTINGENT FACULTY MEMBERS

A good example of why the guidelines just presented are important occurs when new adjunct and full-time temporary members are introduced to the institution. Many colleges and universities require (or at least expect) contingent faculty members to attend the same orientation and onboarding activities that they provide tenure-track faculty members. In some ways, that requirement is logical. Every new employee has to complete paperwork for tax purposes and record keeping. The paperwork that faculty members must complete often doesn't entirely overlap what staff members must complete, so it seems to make sense for all faculty members to have the same onboarding procedures, regardless of their status.

Nevertheless, remember the problems discussed in Chapter 3 about common practices in faculty orientation and onboarding. The paperwork "death march" and long series of presentations, which are intended to be welcoming but are frequently dull and repetitious, actually work against a school's faculty retention goals. That unfortunate fact is doubly true for part-time faculty members who have to sit through presentations that are not entirely relevant to them (such as sessions on benefits that are only available to full-time or continuing employees) and who usually aren't compensated for doing so. If you want to increase the likelihood that you'll retain your best contingent faculty members, a different approach is needed.

The following are some guidelines for making the onboarding and orientation of contingent faculty members more effective:

- Minimize the amount of paperwork these faculty members need to complete, permitting them to provide as much information as possible online and on their own schedules. For documents that need to be completed in person, allow people to drop by the human resources office anytime at their own convenience.
- Invite contingency faculty members to other orientation activities, particularly social events, but make it clear that their participation in these events is strictly optional. No one expects or requires them to attend.
- For orientation information that is essential, put these sessions online in formats that the faculty members can complete whenever they like. Make these sessions *competency based* rather than *time on task based* so that more experienced faculty members who already know most of the information can complete them quickly. For example, don't include a lot of videos that the faculty member has to watch before moving through the orientation. Make videos either optional or mandatory only if certain questions are answered wrong on the program's periodic quizzes.
- Instead of a mandatory orientation program, consider providing an online faculty resource database that contingent faculty members can consult when and if necessary.
- If orientation activities are required, regardless of whether they are in person or online, give adjunct faculty members who complete them some sort of compensation. The compensation doesn't have to be in the form of salary. Those who complete the program successfully could be given a gift certificate to the campus bookstore or dining facilities, a free parking pass, or some similar benefit.
- Offer at least some professional development opportunities to contingent faculty members who remain at the institution for a minimum of three years. These opportunities might include some travel funding or registration fees for local workshops, or they may include an invitation to participate in any faculty development programs sponsored by the academic department, the provost's office, or the office of human resources.
- Some contingent faculty members may not know their way around campus very well. And since they often don't work on campus all day every day, they may not develop a sense of where various buildings are located as quickly as other faculty members do. For those who are interested, offer a tour. The admissions office and public relations office are used to giving campus tours to visitors and prospective students. They may well

have staff members who can assist you in helping contingent faculty members feel more at home.
- Although contingent faculty members may not qualify for certain benefits, they may want to hear about where they might find the lowest-cost health insurance that's available to them, how to open their own individual retirement account, where daycare is available in the area, and similar topics. Your school's human resources office probably has information about these matters that would be valuable to contingent faculty. So, an optional session that provides an overview of this kind might be welcome to part-time and temporary full-time employees.

In a study conducted on different approaches to providing orientation programs to adjunct faculty members, Katie Fischer, Sara Kellogg, and Deb Erickson recommended that it's important to reflect on how robust your overall faculty development program is. If the program already addresses topics such as effective pedagogical techniques for different class sizes and learning platforms; developing an appropriate student-teacher relationship; the specific technology used by the institution (such as the email and classroom management systems); special aspects of the school's mission, values, and culture (particularly significant at schools with a religious mission); and similar topics, the general orientation can be very brief. If a well-developed faculty development program doesn't exist, the orientation can be longer, but even then it should have a specific focus like mission and values or effective pedagogy. An endless series of people introducing themselves is unlikely to be of much value (Fischer, Kellogg, and Erickson, 2020). It would be far better to have a shorter program with a clear purpose and substantive content.

CONTINUING SUPPORT FOR CONTINGENT FACULTY

The right kind of orientation program for contingent faculty members can help build faculty loyalty and engagement from the very beginning of their service to the institution. But by itself it's not enough. It's also important to create a system that provides the kind of support adjunct and full-time temporary faculty members need throughout their employment. And that support may not be exactly the same as what tenure-track faculty members need.

As we've already seen, any faculty member who is paid a less-than-full-time salary needs to be given options about the degree to which he or she wants to be involved in meetings and shared governance. And if faculty development is an expectation for continued employment, then it needs to be provided in a flexible format so that training can be completed on a schedule that works for people who are often juggling multiple jobs as well as responsibilities at home. But beyond flexibility, what else should one expect to find in a successful support program for contingent faculty members?

To begin with, we should recognize that a higher proportion of contingent faculty members have more extensive experience outside of higher education than do tenure-line faculty members. While neither group should be seen as monolithic, a substantial number of tenure-line faculty members follow a fairly straight path in their career development from undergraduate education to graduate school to postdoctoral work to employment at a college or university. That same pattern can be found among contingent faculty members, but a greater proportion of them have a history of professional experience that interrupts this flow.

For some contingent faculty members, that interruption was a necessity; inability to find a full-time tenure-track position caused them to pursue other career paths. For others, employment outside of higher education was a choice. What this means is that a valuable source of expertise is often overlooked by faculty development programs. While it's not at all uncommon to see seminars and workshops on how to incorporate your *research* into one's teaching, it's relatively rare to see professional development opportunities on how to incorporate *professional experience* into one's teaching.

As a result, at least some contingent faculty members are left believing that their professional experience isn't valued by the institution or that, in order to find ways of how to enhance teaching through practical examples and experience in the field, they have to figure out pedagogical strategies by themselves. In either case, the result can be faculty disengagement and attrition.

It's important to reiterate that academic leaders shouldn't assume that contingent faculty members have no interest in research or that their career paths aren't similar to those of tenure-line faculty members. It's just that administrators shouldn't assume that the needs and career trajectories of contingent faculty members are always *identical* to those of their tenure-line faculty members. Effective faculty development programs are those that provide options: options in format, options in timing, and options in content. The key questions that faculty development directors need to ask are:

- What strengths and areas of expertise are members of the faculty already likely to have?
- How can we help faculty members use those strengths and areas of expertise even more effectively?
- What challenges are at least some members of the faculty likely to have?
- How can we better help those faculty members overcome, compensate for, or deal with those challenges?

Second, support for contingent faculty members shouldn't overlook the resources that already exist. New Faculty Majority (NFM) is an organization, founded in 2009, that provides advocacy for part-time and temporary faculty members. Through its website and programs, administrators can learn what the actual needs and concerns of contingent faculty members are and then adapt their programs and policies accordingly. The group has a specific policy agenda that can be useful for understanding the changes that need to be made in higher education to improve the quality of education, retain highly valuable contingent faculty members, and adapt to the new reality of how higher education must be provided in a changing world. As the motto of NFM states, "Faculty working conditions are student learning conditions" (NFM Policy Agenda, n.d.).

Another resource that already exists for administrators is the Part-Time Faculty Integration Model developed by John Roueche, Suanne Roueche, and Mark Milliron (1996). This model takes what a part-time faculty member brings to his or her position, builds on that through institutional strategies, and then measures three kinds of results: personal outcomes, organizational outcomes, and degree of institutional identification.

According to Roueche, Roueche, and Milliron, what a part-time faculty member brings to an institution includes

> his or her unique history, personal expectations, and motivations for the position. For example, the part-timer hoping for a full-time opportunity brings certain motivations and expectations to the position that a moonlighter might not bring (such as, "If I do well, I will be hired full-time"). (Roueche, Roueche, and Milliron, 1996, 37)

Those factors are then affected by how the school develops and treats the faculty members, a group of behaviors that the authors term *concertive strategies* including socialization, communication, and participation in such matters as curricular development. The result of this interaction is then personal and professional growth, organizational results such as better decision-making, and an increase or decrease in the degree to which the faculty member is loyal to and identifies with the institution (Roueche, Roueche, and Milliron, 1996).

What the Part-Time Faculty Integration Model means for academic leaders is that if they wish to retain and make the best use of their part-time faculty members they need to do a better job in three areas:

1. They need to evaluate not only the credentials and professional experience of incoming contingent faculty members as discussed earlier, but also their expectations and motivations. A professional development opportunity that positions a contingent faculty member for joining the

ranks of the tenure-track faculty is a wasted effort if that is not what the person wants or expects. Conversely, if someone *does* see his or her future as a tenure-line faculty member, then faculty development opportunities should be provided, not to guarantee that result, but to increase its degree of possibility.
2. They need to be flexible in the amount of socialization, communication, participation, and training they offer contingent faculty members. Some part-time and temporary faculty members want to be included in all social events, be informed about everything going on in their programs and at their institutions, have the same voice in policy matters as other faculty members do, and be given access to professional development activities. Others either don't want or don't have time for any of that. Still others want certain opportunities (such as communication and participation) but not others (such as socialization and professional development). If academic leaders are aware of the expectations of their contingent faculty members, they can do a better job in providing each person with the right opportunities.
3. They need to assess the impact of their decisions. If faculty engagement studies are done, the results need to be cross-tabulated so that it's possible to determine whether different groups (such as part-time, full-time temporary, and full-time tenure-line faculty members) feel different degrees of institutional attachment. Just as an academic leader would want to know whether women are having a different experience from men or minority faculty members are having a different experience from majority faculty members, so is it important to know where there is variation in faculty engagement and institutional loyalty based on employment status.

Third, both formative and summative evaluation processes should reflect the realities of being a contingent faculty member. Faculty evaluation criteria are long overdue for an overhaul at many institutions. Even though faculty responsibilities have grown to include such duties as student recruitment, fundraising, and outcomes assessment, most systems of faculty evaluation still only reward professors for their work in teaching, research, and service. While this problem exists for all faculty members, it is particularly severe for contingent faculty members whose responsibilities may be quite different from those of their tenure-eligible colleagues.

At some institutions, part-time and full-time temporary faculty members aren't eligible for promotion at all. At others, policies do exist for promotion to such ranks as senior instructor, university instructor, or regents instructor, but the criteria remain only slightly adapted from those used for the promotion of tenure-track faculty members. It can thus be all but impossible to get promoted if doing so requires significant activity in teaching, research, and service but you're never given any research support or allowed to serve on any committees.

Retaining contingent faculty members thus requires institutions to consider what it is that these members of the community actually do and what constitutes appropriate levels of achievement in those areas. If all a contingent faculty member is allowed to do is teach, how does an applicant for promotion to the rank of senior instructor document excellence in teaching? Is it based solely on student course evaluations, peer reviews, and length of service, or are there other indicators a contingent faculty member can use to support his or her success in teaching?

Even more than other ranks of faculty members, contingent faculty members should be promoted on the basis of portfolio evaluation, not numbers of articles they've published or the size of the grants they've received. A portfolio that demonstrates growth in teaching would include such documents as

- A statement of teaching philosophy so that reviewers can develop a sense not only of what the applicant has taught but why he or she taught it that way
- Annotated samples of syllabi from five or more years accompanied by samples of current syllabi so that reviewers can better understand how the applicant has developed as a teacher
- Examples of course materials that indicate the creativity and effectiveness of the applicant's pedagogical approaches
- Scans of graded materials (with student information redacted) so that reviewers can gain a sense of the type of advice the applicant provides to students
- Lists of intended course outcomes with evidence that those outcomes have been achieved so that reviewers can judge the effectiveness of the applicant's instructional methods

Other examples of appropriate materials for inclusion in a teaching portfolio can be found in Peter Seldin, J. Elizabeth Miller, and Clement Seldin's *The Teaching Portfolio* (2010) and Patricia Rieman and Jeanne Okrasinski's *Creating Your Teaching Portfolio* (2007). This portfolio approach to evaluation helps overcome the tendency that promotion committees often have to merely count items on a curriculum vitae and to overemphasize the importance of student course evaluations, neither of which may be the best indicator of whether a contingent faculty member has actually excelled at teaching.

Finally, in order for contingent faculty members to feel at home, academic leaders need to make sure that they *have* a home. If they aren't assigned an office, they need somewhere to hold office hours, meet informally with students, and simply go between their classes. A lounge for contingent faculty seems like a small thing, but imagine how it must feel when even such a small thing isn't regarded as a worthwhile investment by an administrator.

CONCLUSION

This chapter began with the recognition that administrators who try to offer what they think contingent faculty members need often find themselves in a double bind. If they try to treat contingent faculty members exactly the same as tenure-line faculty members, they run the risk of imposing expectations for time commitments that the contingent faculty member can't afford and isn't compensated for. If they try to treat contingent faculty members differently than tenure-line faculty members, they run the risk of being perceived as regarding contingent faculty members as second-class citizens or disenfranchising them.

The fact is that, like all faculty members, contingent faculty members aren't homogeneous. The best way to retain them is to *ask them* what they need, want, and expect and to realize that the answer may well be different for each individual. At the same time, academic leaders should be working hard at their institutions to change policies that take advantage of contingent faculty members and cause them to become disengaged.

Most importantly of all, academic leaders should do everything in their power to make sure that comparable work is comparably rewarded. Those who are not on tenure lines may have different responsibilities from those who are, and compensation levels can reflect this difference. But when adjunct and temporary full-time faculty members are paid the merest fraction of what institutions pay their tenure-line faculty members, it can come as no surprise that some of their best teachers will seek opportunities elsewhere.

KEY POINTS IN THIS CHAPTER

- Contingent faculty members (i.e., adjuncts and those who work on part-time or full-time temporary contracts) have become an increasingly important segment of the higher education workforce.
- Nevertheless, salary levels, benefits, and opportunities for contingent faculty members lag far behind those of their tenure-eligible counterparts. The result is a high rate of contingent faculty attrition.
- The career paths, life situations, and needs of contingent faculty members are at least as diverse as the needs of those on continuing contracts.

For that reason, academic leaders need to consult with each contingent faculty member about his or her individual expectations and desires.
- Faculty development programs with sessions on how to use professional experience as a basis for course content and enhancement can be valuable to many contingent faculty members.
- The Part-Time Faculty Integration Model developed by Roueche, Roueche, and Milliron in 1996 can provide academic leaders with a structure for promoting the retention of contingent faculty members and assessing the success of their strategies.
- Institutions should provide opportunities for contingent faculty members to be promoted, as well as promotion criteria that reflect the reality of how contingent faculty members serve the college or university.

REFERENCES

Background Facts on Contingent Faculty Positions: American Association of University Professors. (n.d.). https://www.aaup.org/issues/contingency/background-facts.

Fischer, K., Kellogg, S., & Erickson, D. (2020). Onboarding adjunct faculty: Two institutional models and lessons learned. *The Department Chair. 31*(1), 8–10.

Lederman, D. (2019). The faculty shrinks, but tilts to full-time. *Inside Higher Ed.* https://www.insidehighered.com/news/2019/11/27/federal-data-show-proportion-instructors-who-work-full-time-rising.

NFM Policy Agenda. (n.d.). http://www.newfacultymajority.info/nfm-advocacy/nfm-policy-agenda/.

Rieman, P. L., Okrasinski, J., & Rieman, P. L. (2007). *Creating your teaching portfolio: Presenting your professional best* (2nd ed.). Boston, MA: McGraw-Hill Higher Education.

Roueche, J. E., Roueche, S. D., & Milliron, M. D. (1996). Identifying the strangers: Exploring part-time faculty integration in American community colleges. *Community College Review. 23*(4), 33–48.

Seldin, P., Miller, J. E., & Seldin, C. A. (2010). *The teaching portfolio: A practical guide to improved performance and promotion/tenure decisions* (4th ed.). San Francisco, CA: Jossey-Bass.

RESOURCES

Baron-Nixon, L. (2007). *Connecting non full-time faculty to institutional mission: A guidebook for college/university administrators and faculty developers.* Sterling, VA: Stylus.

Beach, A. L., Sorcinelli, M. D., Austin, A. E., & Rivard, J. K. (2016). *Faculty development in the age of evidence: Current practices, future imperatives.* Sterling, VA: Stylus.

Chapin, J. R. (2018). Welcoming your new adjunct faculty members. *The Department Chair. 29*(1), 16–17.

Keller, L. M. R. (2015). *Adjunct faculty engagement: Connections in pursuit of student success in community colleges.* Ed.D. thesis at Northeastern University. https://repository.library.northeastern.edu/files/neu:rx917q27n/fulltext.pdf.

Pearch, W. J., & Marutz, L. (2005). Retention of adjunct faculty in community colleges. *Community College Enterprise. 11*(1), 29–44.

Chapter 7

Creating a Culture of Hiring and Retaining the Best

As should be clear to every reader by now, the answer to the question, "How can I better retain my best faculty members?" isn't simply "Do this," whatever "this" might happen to be. Faculty retention has to be addressed through a multipronged approach, and doing so requires academic leaders to do one of the hardest things they can do in higher education: change the culture from what it has been to what it should be.

The paradox of higher education has always been that, for a profession that regularly recommends how individuals, organizations, and processes need to change, it is extraordinarily change averse. Despite advances in technology and improved understanding of how students learn, many classrooms are still being designed in the same way they were designed several centuries ago, and many professors still teach the way in which generations of professors taught before them. Anyone who has tried to promote constructive, sustainable change in higher education understands just how many obstacles the system imposes. It's no wonder that many new professors who are filled with enthusiasm for improving how classes are taught and institutions are run find that enthusiasm drained from them entirely by the time they apply for their first promotion.

Retaining high-performing college professors will remain an overwhelming challenge, particularly for schools that are underfunded or regarded as less than prestigious, until there's a change in the culture of how faculty members are hired, assigned duties, and rewarded. As an academic leader, you can't change that culture overnight, but there are meaningful steps that you can take right now to initiate the long process of change that will be required.

A longitudinal study of faculty workload conducted by KerryAnn O'Meara, Audrey Jaeger, Joya Misra, Courtney Lennartz, and Alexandra Kuvaeva indicated that a few easily implemented practices led to a demonstrable decrease

in workload inequity, one of the major causes of faculty attrition. The interventions that produced statistically significant improvements were:

> (a) a workshop on implicit bias and how it can shape divisions of labor, (b) arming department teams with tools to create and display faculty workload activity dashboards, (c) using dashboards to identify equity issues and sharing work practices and policies to mitigate bias and proactively design for equity, and (d) an optional professional development webinar series on aligning time and priorities as a faculty member. At the conclusion of this 18-month project, the intervention measurably improved one work practice associated with workload satisfaction—having transparent data on faculty work activities available for department faculty, and likewise improved several conditions related to workload equity such as awareness of implicit bias and commitment among faculty to work being fair. (O'Meara, Jaeger, Misra, Lennartz, and Kuvaeva, 2018)

In short, when academic leaders understood how implicit bias could lead to workload inequity, they became aware of their own unconscious tendencies in time to correct mistakes they would otherwise have made. When accurate data about workload became publicly available, it was easier for adjustments to be made that caused work assignments to become fairer. When faculty members had an opportunity to receive training in time management, they were able to shift their own workload priorities in ways that increased their productivity and levels of institutional satisfaction.

Becoming more transparent about workload and offering workshops on implicit bias and time management aren't onerous or expensive tasks. In fact, they represent practices that academic leaders should already be doing, not only to improve faculty retention, but also to make their programs and institutions the type of fair and open work environments they already claim them to be.

Offering the right kind of training shouldn't be underestimated. One study conducted in Pakistan showed that opportunities for learning that led to personal and professional growth had an even greater effect on faculty retention than did salary increases (Zeeshan Mubarak, Wahab, and Khan, 2012). Make no mistake about it: Paying faculty members fair and appropriate salaries is important. But salary expectations are also never-ending. Colleges and universities will never have sufficient resources to pay everyone what they want and feel they deserve.

Investments in professional development, however, are easier to control and have a more immediate impact. By discovering what type of workshops and webinars faculty members want, these programs can be provided either by in-house experts or by professional leadership training companies at a rate that even small programs and institutions can afford.

In addition, this book has introduced a wide range of other options that are available to academic leaders. While some of these suggestions, such as adjusting the criteria for faculty evaluation and developing new ranks beyond the level of full professor, involve long-term changes to systems and cultures, other strategies can be implemented almost immediately. If you're an academic leader who wants to improve faculty retention in your program or at your school, what can you do *next week*?

WHAT DEPARTMENT CHAIRS CAN DO

Perhaps the most important action that department chairs can take to promote the retention of their best faculty members is to check in with them regularly and express their appreciation for what they do to advance the program. Doing so requires absolutely no financial outlay whatsoever, but it can have a major impact on reducing faculty attrition.

The frequent refrain that academic leaders need to be more data-driven in their approaches sometimes gives department chairs the notion that the interpersonal aspects of their jobs are insignificant. As long as they track the data and adjust their strategies accordingly, some chairs assume they're doing their jobs. Nothing can be further from the truth. The interpersonal skills of a department chair are integral to the success of the program. Conflicts aren't resolved, visions aren't communicated, and faculty members aren't engaged through data alone. The department chair actually has to say to faculty members—sincerely and one-on-one—"I really value the contributions you're making to the success of the program. Is there anything I can do to make your job easier or better in some way?"

Chairs are sometimes reluctant to ask this question because they assume that they'll be inundated with requests for higher salaries and more funding for research and travel. Those requests may well be made. But when that occurs, the chair has an opportunity to explain the realities of departmental budgeting and to suggest some of the *other* ways in which excellent faculty members can be rewarded, such as those discussed in Chapters 1, 4, and 6. The conversation allows the chair to discover what the faculty member actually needs and expects, which is better than having the person simply suffer in silence because he or she thinks the chair doesn't care. By explaining budgetary realities and expressing a willingness to do what's possible, chairs increase their level of leadership transparency and gain insights they may not have gained if they hadn't asked a few questions.

It may also be assumed by chairs that they don't need to express regular appreciation to their best faculty members because these people already know how much they're valued or would find such expressions of gratitude childish and unprofessional. That assumption is almost certainly false. Many of our best faculty members are starving for recognition and would be grateful for a few supportive words from the chair. Moreover, even if chairs believe that they're already expressing appreciation frequently, the perception of their faculty members is likely to be quite different. It doesn't hurt (and will probably help more than you might believe) to start being more proactive in thanking people for the individual contributions they make but probably believe are unrecognized.

Expressing gratitude more often may help you as well as the faculty member. The psychologist Sonja Lyubomirsky found that thanking just *one more person a day* beyond what someone would ordinarily do increased the happiness not just of the one who was thanked but also of the person doing the thanking (Lyubomirsky, 2007, 96–97). The result can then be exponential. If you're happier and more engaged, you'll create an atmosphere that will make it easier for people in your program to become happier and more engaged. That, in turn, should increase your own job satisfaction, and the cycle will continue.

WHAT DEANS AND PROVOSTS CAN DO

The most important thing that deans and provosts can do immediately to improve faculty retention is to see themselves primarily as advocates for the faculty and to make it clear to others that advocacy is their most important role. A barrier often exists between faculty and chairs on one side and deans and provosts on the other because the latter groups are regarded more as *judges* than as advocates. A common perception, even if it's rarely articulated, is that deans and provosts are obstacles that can get in the way of what the faculty and chairs want. Once you accept a position as dean or provost, many of the people who report to you will see you as one of "them," not one of "us."

That may not at all be your self-perception. You may have risen (and probably did rise) through the ranks of the faculty to your current position and regard yourself much more as a faculty member than an administrator. Whether you realize it or not, many of the people who report to you don't see you that way. Unless you intentionally and repeatedly act as an advocate for your people and programs, many faculty members simply won't believe that you "feel their pain."

In order to reduce faculty attrition, deans need to make it clear that their most fundamental job is to advocate for those in their college, and provosts need to make it clear that their most fundamental job is to advocate for the academic side of the institution. They do so by asking people what they want and need (exactly as chairs should do); listen to what people say; act assertively to satisfy the needs that can appropriately be met; and report to faculty, staff, and chairs on what they've done. They can't say they're advocates unless they *act* as advocates, and they won't be recognized as advocates unless they repeatedly *describe* themselves that way.

If department chairs have a temptation to see the charge to be data-driven as a mandate to become data-obsessed, deans and provosts have a temptation to elevate data obsession to an entirely new level of data worship. That temptation is understandable. Presidents, boards, legislatures, and accrediting bodies all want to ensure that decisions are based on clear and accurate information. But gathering and interpreting information can't be the only task that deans and provosts regard as important. They also need to invest in people because failure to do so leads to attrition of students, faculty, and staff, and attrition never makes the data look good.

There is a stereotype that many employees have of the boss as a taskmaster, not an ally. People who reach the mid- and upper levels of administration sometimes believe that stereotype doesn't exist in higher education because of such concepts as collegiality and the community of scholars. But administrators who work in a unionized environment are disabused of that allusion far sooner than many administrators who work at schools without collective bargaining. If you want to understand how faculty members view administrators, sit across the table from them in contract negotiations.

Nevertheless, there's no reason why that divide has to become a chasm. Include faculty representatives on administrative councils and policy committees. Go to department meetings, not to make a presentation, but to listen. Remember what it was like to hear "Students come first!" and "Students are our top priority!" and to wonder as a faculty member exactly where you fit on that list of priorities. And then go out and advocate on behalf of those who still wonder.

WHAT UPPER ADMINISTRATORS AND GOVERNING BOARDS CAN DO

Relatively few members of governing boards have worked professionally in higher education. Increasingly, presidents and chancellors are also being selected from fields outside of the academic world. The result can sometimes be a disconnect between how boards and CEOs view higher education and how faculty members and other administrators view it.

As this author, along with development professional Dianne Reeves, described this difference of perspective,

> Board members sometimes believe that shared governance in higher education is an inefficient process that takes far too long to make easy decisions, consumes resources for layers of administration that would be better spent on teaching and research and responds poorly to the changing needs of society. . . . They may find the very concepts of tenure and academic freedom to be antithetical to their philosophy of keeping organizations lean and cost-effective. Tenure, which is regarded by faculty members as essential for the protection of academic freedom, may be interpreted by board members as job protection regardless of one's level of competence. Academic freedom, which faculty members view as vital to the open exchange of ideas, may be regarded by board members as the license to speak without accountability. Those differences in outlook sometimes cause serious miscommunication between the academic world and the world of the advisory or governing board. (Buller and Reeves, 2018, 93)

For example, when presidents and members of the governing board say things like, "The students are our customers," they're often unaware of how tone deaf such statements sound to faculty members. To a college professor, customers are people who get what they want; students are people who get what they earn. A customer in a diner who demands a double order of eggs and a quadruple order of bacon is likely to get it because "the customer is always right." Students who demand two A+s and four As are only likely to get them if they deserve them.

In a similar way, presidents and governing boards may say such things as, "This university should run more like a business." But faculty members view learning, rather than profit, as a university's "bottom line." The school has to be able to pay its bills, of course. But to most faculty members, the idea that a college or university has failed somehow because its tuition, fees, and grant income didn't far exceed its expenditures is a fundamental misunderstanding of what a college or university actually is.

These misunderstandings can drive faculty attrition. Imagine for a moment that you are a doctor with a patient who's clearly addicted to painkillers. You wouldn't give the patient what he or she wants merely because "the customer is always right." Or imagine that you're a general charged with securing the national defense. You wouldn't see yourself as having failed merely because your units failed to "turn a profit" that year.

Now imagine how you might respond as a doctor whose hospital administrator blamed you for not prescribing those painkillers because "the patients are our customers" or a general whose president blamed you for not ending the year in the black because "this army should be run more like a business." If that is your experience year after year, your level of engagement will almost certainly plummet, and you'll seek work elsewhere or leave your profession entirely.

If upper administrators and governing boards are truly interested in promoting student success and increasing budgetary efficiency, they'll take the problem of faculty attrition seriously. Students are better served by reduced faculty turnover since the better professors get to know their students by working with them in multiple classes, the more they can tailor instruction to the needs of those students and the more compelling their letters of recommendations for those students will be. Budgets are easier to balance when there's reduced faculty turnover since, as was noted earlier, searches are expensive and new hires almost always demand higher salaries than the people they're replacing.

So, in addition to implementing the policy changes recommended elsewhere in this book, presidents and governing boards can start to improve faculty retention—quickly and at no cost whatsoever—by taking steps to see the world through the eyes of the faculty. More than one president or member of a board has complained to a college professor, "You have to see things from my perspective. I'm aware of things that you're not." College professors can make the same demand of presidents and board members. Until both sides take the time to appreciate what the other is trying to accomplish and how certain constraints can make that goal more difficult, faculty attrition is likely to increase.

CONCLUSION

At this point, it must be noted, however, that the recommendations offered so far in this chapter are the *beginnings* of a plan to increase faculty retention. They're not the entire plan. All of the other strategies outlined throughout this book—such as developing new faculty ranks, improving the ways in which faculty members are onboarded, addressing inequities in faculty workload, and so on—are necessary additional steps that administrators and institutions will need to take. Faculty attrition can't be staunched by a "quick fix" or a public relations campaign. It ultimately requires a permanent change in institutional culture.

Perhaps the most important aspect of that changed culture at schools that truly care about faculty retention will be a revised structure for faculty roles and rewards, including clearer criteria for meeting the standards by which college professors are evaluated. The current structure for roles and rewards in place at many institutions is badly out of date. It's based on only the standard academic triad—teaching, research, and service—even though a professor's job these days requires the performance of duties that don't fit into that structure. As academic leaders, we simply can't expect faculty members to help us recruit students, engage in fundraising, promote undergraduate research, and do all the other things that now constitute success as a college professor unless our evaluation criteria change. (See Soomro and Ahmad, 2013.)

The three-legged stool of the old academic triad had its purpose. But it's no longer a valuable technique for recognizing faculty performance and thus promoting faculty retention. At most schools evaluation criteria don't even mention collegiality, and yet the most outstanding faculty members leave our institutions not because of the job itself but because of how others treat them (Cipriano and Buller, 2013). Colleges and universities sometimes shy away from evaluating faculty members for their collegiality because "it seems so subjective" and "isn't it better to have a difficult genius on the faculty than nothing but congenial mediocrities?"

These objections are misguided. Collegiality is a *behavior*, not a personality trait, and institutions evaluate faculty members on their behaviors all the time. Insubordination is a behavior. Failing to keep office hours is a behavior. Treating students with contempt is a behavior. If administrators can evaluate faculty members on those behaviors, subjective though those appraisals may be at times, they can also evaluate faculty members on breaches of collegiality such as treating coworkers with contempt, failing to "step up" when their contributions are needed, and undermining the institution's regular decision-making processes (Cipriano and Buller, 2011; and Cipriano and Buller, 2012).

Making these changes won't be easy. But, as academic leaders, our bookshelves are full of works providing data and offering suggestions about student success. Until we begin to take the professional growth, effective evaluation, and evolving needs of our faculty as seriously as we take the success of our students, retaining our best college professors will remain merely a hope, not an attainable goal.

KEY POINTS IN THIS CHAPTER

- Improving faculty retention requires a multipronged approach. There are steps that academic leaders can take immediately, but ultimately a major change in culture will be necessary.
- That major change in institutional culture should include revised criteria for faculty evaluation, training in implicit bias and how it can affect the way in which supervisors assign duties, better tracking of faculty workload, and professional development training on how best to align time and priorities as a faculty member.

- Academic leaders should also do more to promote collegiality in their units since poor work environments are a leading cause of faculty attrition.
- Department chairs can check in on their best faculty members regularly and express their appreciation for what these faculty members have done to advance the program.
- Deans and provosts can revise how they see their roles, viewing themselves primarily as advocates and making it clear to others that advocacy is their most important responsibility.
- Presidents, chancellors, and governing boards can try harder to see the institution as faculty members see it, not as a hierarchy, but as a "community of scholars" who strive to work together collegially to educate students and advance knowledge.

REFERENCES

Buller, J. L., & Reeves, D. M. (2018). *The five cultures of academic development*. Washington, DC: CASE.

Cipriano, R. E., & Buller, J. L. (2011). Collegiality in faculty personnel decisions: Standards for a definition and objective evaluation. *The Department Chair. 22*(2), 3–4.

Cipriano, R. E., & Buller, J. L. (2012). Rating faculty collegiality. *Change. 44*(2), 45–48.

Cipriano, R. E., & Buller, J. L. (2013). Collegiality and positive relationships. *The Department Chair. 23*(4), 6–8.

Lyubomirsky, S. (2007). *The how of happiness*. New York, NY: Penguin.

O'Meara, K., Jaeger, A., Misra, J., Lennartz, C., & Kuvaeva, A. (2018). Undoing disparities in faculty workloads: A randomized trial experiment. *PLoS ONE. 13*(12), e0207316. https://doi.org/10.1371/journal.pone.0207316.

Soomro, T. R., & Ahmad, R. (2013). Faculty retention in higher education. *International Journal of Higher Education. 2*(2), 147–150.

Zeeshan Mubarak, R., Wahab, Z., & Khan, N. R. (2012). Faculty retention in higher education institutions of Pakistan. *Ricerche di Pedagogia e Didattica/Journal of Theories and Research in Education. 7*(2), 65–78.

RESOURCES

Condon, W. (2016). *Faculty development and student learning: Assessing the connections*. Bloomington, IN: Indiana University Press.

Flaherty, C. (2019). Evening things out. *Inside Higher Ed.* https://www.insidehighered.com/news/2019/01/30/new-research-says-relatively-simple-interventions-are-effective-addressing-faculty.

Harrington, C. (2020). *Ensuring learning: Supporting faculty to improve student success.* Lanham, MD: Rowman & Littlefield.

Index

academia: administrators role in, 37, 38, 97–100; core values of leaders in, 74; culture change in, 95, 102; experience of governing board members outside, 99–100; first day of work in, 25; freedom in, 68; resistance to change of, 95; writing in, 13
academic fraud, 3
academic triad, 101–2
access, to mentor, 12, 18, 28, 41, 49–50
accreditation standards, change in, 71
Adelphi University, 43
adjustment, in responsibilities, 12–13, 44
administrators: data collection and, 99; interpersonal skills of, 97, 99, 103; as obstacles, 98–99, 103; role in faculty retention, 37, 39, 97–100
administrators and faculty, disconnect between, 99–100, 101
advocates, deans and provosts as, 98–99, 103
Affirmative Action, Equal Opportunity contrasted with, 20
Agago, Menna O., 54–55
ambassadors, senior faculty as, 50–51
American Association of University Professors, 38–39, 79

Annual Review of Psychology (journal), 67
apologies, genuine, 74–75
application for other jobs, for counteroffer, 51, 54
associate professors: options for, 45; terminal, 4–5, 9
assumptions, about faculty needs, 15, 21, 97
attrition, faculty, 1, 4, 9, 15, 20
average professors, 4

Barnes, Laura L. B., 54–55
behavior, troubling, 15–16, 102
benefits, of associate professors moving jobs, 45
best practices, of institutions, 17, 26–35, 53
bias, implicit, 96
Black Lives Matter Movement, 20
Blank, Rebecca, 2
Buckingham, Marcus, 67
budget, 97–100; cuts, 1–2; discretionary, 5–6; tenure track, 82
building, of community, 57–58, 99
Buller, Jeffrey, 99–100
burnout, professional, 40

businesses: as hierarchical, 72; universities compared with, 71–72, 100

CAMPOS. *See* Center for the Advancement of Multicultural Perspectives on Science
campus tour, 83–84
career development opportunities, local, 46–47
career path, of contingent faculty, 85, 89
Carnegie Mellon University, 56
case studies, in Faculty First Year sessions, 32
Center for the Advancement of Multicultural Perspectives on Science (CAMPOS), 18–19
central faculty development unit, 70
change: in academic culture, 95, 102; in accreditation standards, 71; in role of faculty, 38–39, 101–2; in vocabulary used toward faculty, 48–49
childcare, 13, 40, 43
choices, for contingent faculty, 80–81
The Chronicle of Higher Education (newspaper & website), 48
clarity, of expectations for faculty, 70–71
classroom, flipped, 32–33
Closing the Engagement Gap (Gebauer & Lowman), 67–68
"Cluster hiring and diversity" (Flaherty), 33
coaching and mentoring, for senior faculty, 49–50, 55, 58, 59, 61
Coffman, Curt, 67
collegiality, 99, 102
Columbia University, 17, 26, 54–56
commencement exercises, community and, 28
committee work: minority faculty and, 16–17; new faculty and, 40–41, 61
community: building, 57–58, 99; cluster hiring for, 33–34; commencement exercises and, 28; faculty as members of, 11, 13, 18; lack of, 14–15; minority, 19–20, 53; orientations and, 26–27, 30
compartmentalization, of knowledge, 27, 73
compensation: non-salary, 6–7, 9, 52–53, 60; for orientation activities, 83
competency-based orientation, 83
comprehensive diversity plan, at universities, 20
compression, salary, 52
concertive strategies, 86–87
confederacy statues, 3
connection, between personal and institutional goals, 75
contingent faculty members: career path of, 85, 89; comparable pay for, 81–82, 89; decline in, 79–80, 89; double bind of, 80–81, 89; expectations of, 86–87; flexibility for, 81, 82, 84, 87; lounge for, 88–89; needs of, 80, 85, 89–90; services for, 84; strengths of, 85; support for, 84–85, 90; work-life balance of, 80, 89–90
contracts, creativity, 70
conversion, of tenure-track positions to adjunct, 79
Coombs, William T., 54–55
core values, of academic leaders, 74
Cornell University, 58
cost considerations, of new faculty, 7, 8, 9, 101
cost saving, faculty development as, 57, 60
Council of Colleges of Arts and Sciences, 20
counteroffers, 52, 60; application to other jobs for, 51, 54
"cramming," ineffectiveness of, 42
creation, of new ranks, 50–51
creativity contracts, 70

cultural: differences, 14; sensitivity training, 17, 22, 55; taxation, 16–17, 22
customers, students as, 100
cuts, budget, 1–2

data, about workload, 96
data collection, administrators and, 99
deans and provosts, as advocates, 98–99, 103
decision-making, of universities, 72
Defining and measuring faculty engagement (Livingston), 69–72
Department of Education, US, 79
differences, cultural, 14
discretionary budget, 5–6
Discretionary Effort Model, 73
diversity, 15, 16, 33; institutions and, 2, 11; recruiting, 11; universities plan for, 20
double bind, of contingent faculty members, 80–81, 89
"dross" faculty, "gold" contrasted with, 4–5

educational program, importance of professor to, 8
"Effects of job-related stress on faculty intention to leave academia" (Barnes, Agago & Coombs), 54–55
employee classification, stratified, 72
employee engagement: faculty engagement contrasted with, 67–68, 71–72, 76; as manipulation, 67, 73; psychological conditions of, 66; satisfaction contrasted with, 66–67; as static, 66; traditional methods of, 73
employees: faculty as, 68; managers left by, 67
employee satisfaction, engagement contrasted with, 66–67
Equal Opportunity, Affirmative Action contrasted with, 20
Erickson, Deb, 84

evaluation: portfolio, 88; promotion criteria for, 18, 71, 88, 96–97, 101–2
exit interviews, 18, 22
expectations, of contingent faculty, 86–87
Experience, First Day, 26
experience of governing board members, outside academia, 99–100

faculty: attrition of, 1, 4, 9, 15, 20; change in role of, 38–39, 101–2; clarity of expectations for, 70–71; contingent, 80, 81–82, 84, 85, 89–90; disconnect between administrators and, 100, 101; as employees, 68; as graded, 41; hiring staff contrasted with, 68; human resources and, 68–69, 76; median time at university, 3–4; as members of community, 11, 13, 18; morale of, 74; needs of, 15, 21, 97; onboarding of, 12, 25–34; sense of community in, 33, 34; simplifying procedures for, 18, 62; social networks of, 32, 35, 56; stars in, 5; turnover rate, 2; as valued, 11, 14–15, 27–28, 47–48; workload reduction of, 69. *See also* contingent faculty; mid-career faculty; minority faculty; new faculty; senior faculty
faculty development program, 32, 58, 59; central unit for, 70; as cost saving, 57, 60; financial incentives for, 40; funding for, 54; misconceptions about, 37–39, 60; for new faculty, 39–40, 56; for senior faculty, 49–51
Faculty Diversity (Moody), 58
faculty engagement, 40, 57, 66; in all roles of job, 69; effective, 73–74; employee engagement contrasted with, 67–68, 71–72, 76; focus on, 42; productivity as sign of, 65, 76; strategies for, 73–74; student engagement contrasted with, 65, 75–76

108

Index

Faculty First Day Welcome, 27, 28, 34
faculty members, contingent: decline in, 79–80
faculty orientation: contingent, 82–84; problems with, 25, 26, 27, 29–30, 34; student orientation contrasted with, 29–30
Faculty Retention Initiative, 53–54
financial incentives, for development programs, 40
financial strain, on new faculty, 39
First, Break All the Rules (Buckingham & Coffman), 67
first day, of academic work, 25
First Year Faculty Experience, 27, 29, 35, 76; case studies in, 32; proposed schedule for, 30–32
Fischer, Katie, 84
The five cultures of academic development (Buller & Reeves), 99–100
fixes, quick, 6, 9, 101
Flaherty, C., 33–34
flexibility, for contingent faculty, 81, 82, 84, 87
flex time, 42–43, 61
flipped classroom, 32–33
fluidity of management, at universities, 72–73
focus, on faculty engagement, 42, 65–66
"For a diverse faculty, start with retention" (Rockquemore), 15
fraud, academic, 3
freedom, academic, 68
frequency, of faculty requests, 8
freshman seminars, 27
Fulbright Fellowships, 47

Gebauer, Julie, 67–68
genuine apologies, 74–75
goals, of mid-career faculty, 48
"gold" faculty, "dross" contrasted with, 4–5
graded, faculty as, 41
graduation ceremonies, 28

Guide to Best Practices in Retentions (Columbia), 26, 55–56

Heath, Chip and Dan, 25–26, 75
help, with childcare, 13, 40, 43
"Helping professors overcome mid-career malaise" (Monaghan), 48
hierarchical, businesses as, 72
Hiller, Joshua, 43–44
Hodge, B., 3
human resources, faculty and, 68–69, 76

identification, of employees with jobs, 66
"Identifying the strangers" (Roueche, Roueche & Milliron), 86
"The impact of turnover on the organization" (Price), 54–55
implicit bias, 96
incentives, for faculty retention, 46
informal leadership positions, 46–47
information overload, 29–30, 35
infrastructure, for retention, 12–13
Inside Higher Ed (website), 44
institutions: best practices of, 17, 26–35, 53; diversity in, 2, 11; loyalty to, 42, 61, 62, 65, 75; shared values of, 70
interpersonal skills, of administrators, 97, 99, 103
interviews, exit, 18, 22
intrinsic motivation, 7
investments, one-time, 6–7, 53–54
isolation, in minority faculty members, 14–15

Jaeger, Audrey, 95–96
jobs, identification of employees with, 66
job satisfaction, 17, 66, 76
John Deere First Day Experience, 26

Kahn, William, 66
Kellogg, Sara, 84
Khamis-Dakwar, Reem, 43–44

knowledge, compartmentalization of, 27, 73
Kuvaeva, Alexandra, 95–96

lack, of community, 14–15
leadership, with transparency, 74
leadership positions, informal, 46–47, 61
leave of absence, unpaid, 47, 52
legacy, of senior faculty, 49
Lennartz, Courtney, 95–96
"Let 'em Leave Philosophy," 7–8
LGBTQIA+, 19
Livingston, Jennifer, 69–72
load, teaching, 54–55
local career development opportunities, 46–47
lounge, for contingent faculty, 88–89
Lowman, Don, 67–68
loyalty, institutional, 42, 61, 62, 65, 75
Lyubomirsky, Sonja, 98

mangers, employees leaving, 67
manipulation, employee engagement as, 67, 73
Manjounes, Cindy, 45
marketable, strong faculty as, 9
Matthew, Patricia, 16
median time at university, of faculty members, 3–4
medical school faculty attrition, 3
mentor, access to, 12, 18, 28, 41, 49–50
mentorship network, 56, 57, 59
Mercado-Lopez, Larissa, 19–20, 21
mid-career crisis, 46
mid-career faculty: goals of, 48; needs of, 44–49, 61; new faculty contrasted with, 45; retention of, 45–46, 58; shift to administration, 45–46
Milliron, Mark, 86
minority faculty, 53; committee work and, 16–17; isolation of, 14–15; resources for, 20, 22; retention of, 3, 11–22; support for, 19–20, 22; visibility of, 21; workload shift of, 16, 17
misconceptions, about faculty development, 37–39
Misra, Joya, 95
Monaghan, Peter, 48
Moody, JoAnne, 58
morale, of faculty, 74
motivation, intrinsic, 7
moving jobs, benefit of, 45

National Endowment for the Humanities (NEH), 47
National Science Foundation, 2
National Survey of Student Engagement, 65
needs: of contingent faculty, 80, 85, 89–90; of mid-career faculty, 44–49, 61; of new faculty, 39–44, 59; of senior faculty, 49–51
NEH. *See* National Endowment for the Humanities
network, mentorship, 56, 57, 59
new faculty: committee work and, 40–41, 61; cost considerations of, 7, 8, 9, 101; financial strain on, 39; mid-career contrasted with, 45; needs of, 39–44, 59; plan for, 41–42, 59, 61; professional identity of, 42; work-life balance of, 39, 42
New Faculty Majority (NFM), 86
new interests, for senior faculty, 50
new ranks, creation of, 50–51
NFM. *See* New Faculty Majority
non-salary compensation, 6–7, 9, 52–53, 60

obstacles, view of administrators as, 98–99, 103
offer: of resources, 15, 17, 42, 58; of smaller raise, 52
office hours, virtual, 44
O'Meara, KerryAnn, 95–96
onboarding, of faculty, 12, 25–34

"Onboarding adjunct faculty" (Fischer, Kellogg & Erickson), 84
one-time investments, 6–7, 53–54, 60
options: for associate professors, 45; for professional development, 74, 83, 90, 96
orientation: activities compensation for, 83; community and, 26–27; competency-based, 83; past assemblies, 27

paperwork timing, shift in, 29, 82–83
Part-Time Faculty Integration Model, 86, 90
part-time faculty member, as problematic term, 79
path forward, for contingent faculty, 81
personal and institutional goals, connection between, 75
Phillips, Susan D., 33
Philosophy, of Let 'Em Leave, 7–8
plan, for new faculty, 41–42, 59, 61
POD Network, 37
policies, tenure stop-clock, 13
portfolio evaluation, 88
potential, of contingent faculty, 81
The Power of Moments (Heath & Heath), 25–26, 75
Price, James L., 54–55
problematic term, part-time faculty member as, 79
problems: with faculty orientation, 25; proactive responses to, 18; with tenure stop-clock policies, 43–44
procedures, simplifying, 18, 62
productivity, as sign of faculty engagement, 65, 76
professional experience, teaching and, 85
professors: average, 4; dross gold contrasted with, 4–5; educational program importance of, 8; traditional divisions of, 5, 61; transition from graduate student to, 12

program, faculty development, 32, 56, 58, 59
promotions: "cramming" ineffective for, 42; evaluation criteria for, 18, 71, 88, 96–97, 101–2
provosts, as advocates, 98–99, 103
psychological conditions, of employee engagement, 66
public and private recognition, of faculty, 6, 58, 59, 97–98

quick fixes, for faculty retention, 6, 9, 101, 102

reassigned time, 6, 55
recognition of faculty, public and private, 6, 58, 59, 97–98
recruiting: diverse faculty, 11; retention contrasted with, 12, 21, 22
reduced service obligation, 6
reduction, of faculty workload, 69
Reeves, Dianne, 99–100
requests, frequency of faculty, 8
research support, 13, 41
resistance to change, of academia, 95
resources, offers of, 15, 17, 42, 58; for minority faculty, 20, 22
resources, training, 47
responses to problems, proactive, 18
responsibilities, adjustment to, 12–13, 44
restructuring, of workload, 69–70, 76, 95–96
retention, of faculty, 1–4, 8; incentives for, 46; infrastructure for, 12; mid-career faculty and, 45–46, 58; minority faculty members and, 3, 11–23; quick fixes for, 6, 9, 101, 102; recruiting contrasted with, 12, 21, 22; retention of students contrasted with, 27; role of administrators in, 37, 39, 97–100; role of cluster hiring in, 33–34, 35; success indicators of, 55

retention of students, faculty retention contrasted with, 27, 34
retirement, transition to, 50, 55, 61
rights, tenure, 1, 39–40, 58, 59
Rockquemore, Kerry Ann, 15
role of academic administrators, in faculty retention, 37, 39, 97–100
role of cluster hiring, in faculty retention, 33–34, 35
Romero, Aldemaro, 20–21
Roueche, John and Suanne, 86, 90

salary, 2, 5, 8, 18, 43
satisfaction, with job, 17, 76
scarce resources, time and money as, 39–40, 60
scheduling, of development programs, 40
Science (journal), 3–4
senior faculty: as ambassadors, 50–51; legacy of, 49–50; as mentors, 49–50, 55, 58, 59, 61; needs of, 49; new interests for, 50, 55–56
sense of community, within faculty, 33, 34
service obligation, reduced, 6
services, for contingent faculty, 84
shared values, of institution, 70
shift, in paperwork timing, 29, 82–83
shift to administration, of mid-career faculty, 45–46
smaller raise, offer of, 52, 60
social identity theory, 66
social networks, of faculty, 32, 35, 56
social support, 13, 59
solutions: faculty retention systemic, 5, 20; for work-life challenges, 6, 48, 56, 60
staff hiring, faculty hiring contrasted with, 68
star faculty, 5–7
statues, confederacy, 3
strategies: concertive, 86–87; faculty engagement, 73
stratified employee classification, 72

strengths, of contingent faculty, 85
strong faculty, as marketable, 9
student engagement, faculty engagement contrasted with, 65, 75–76
Student First Year Experience, 30
student orientation, faculty orientation contrasted with, 29–30, 34
students: as customers, 100; as valued, 27
study, of faculty development funding, 54
success indicators, for faculty retention, 55, 88
support: for contingent faculty, 84–85, 90; for minority faculty, 19–20, 22; research, 13, 41; social, 13, 59
systemic solutions, for faculty retentions, 5, 20

taxation, cultural, 16–17, 22
teaching: load, 54–55; professional experience and, 85
teaching profession: burnout in, 40; development options for, 42, 83, 90, 96; identity of new faculty in, 42
tenure rights, 1, 5, 39–40, 58, 60; budget for, 82
tenure stop-clock policies, 13; problems with, 43–44
tenure-track positions to adjunct, conversion of, 79
terminal associate professors, 4–5, 9
"The problems with pausing the tenure clock" (Khamis-Dakwar & Hiller), 44
time: flex, 42–43, 61; reassigned, 6, 55; of transition, 25–26
time and money, as scarce resources, 39–40, 60
tour, of campus, 83–84
traditional: divisions of professors as, 5, 61; methods of employee engagement as, 73
training: cultural sensitivity, 17, 22, 55; resources for, 47

transition, 25–26, 30, 45; from graduate student to professor, 12; graduation as, 28; to retirement, 50, 55, 61
transparency, leadership with, 74
triad, academic, 101–2
troubling behavior, 15–16, 102
turnover rate, faculty, 2

UC Davis. *See* University of California, Davis
UNC. *See* University of North Carolina
"UNC faculty chair stepping down" (Hodge), 3
"Undoing disparities in faculty workloads" (O'Meara, Jaeger, Misra, Lennartz & Kuvaeva), 95–96
United States (U. S.), Education Department, 79
universities: businesses compared with, 71–72, 100; comprehensive diversity plan at, 20; decision-making at, 72; fluidity of management at, 72–73
University of California, Davis, 18, 19
University of North Carolina (UNC), 2–3
University of Washington (UW), 53–54
University of Wisconsin-Madison (UW), 1

unpaid leave of absence, 47, 52
U. S. *See* United States
UW. *See* University of Washington; University of Wisconsin-Madison

valued: faculty being, 8, 11, 14–15, 27–28, 47–48; students being, 27
virtual office hours, 44
visibility, of minority faculty, 21
vocabulary used toward faculty, change in, 48–49

Walden University, 45
"What Do Faculty Do?" (American Association of University Professors), 38–39
"What is faculty diversity worth to a university?" (Matthew), 16
work-life balance: of contingent faculty, 80, 89–90; of new faculty, 39, 42
work-life challenges, solutions to, 6, 48, 56, 60
workload, data about, 96
workload, restructuring of, 69–70, 76, 95–96
workload shift, for minority faculty, 16, 17
writing, academic, 13

About the Author

Jeffrey L. Buller is a senior partner in ATLAS: Academic Training, Leadership, & Assessment Services. He has served in administrative positions ranging from department chair to vice president for academic affairs at four very different institutions: Loras College, Georgia Southern University, Mary Baldwin College, and Florida Atlantic University. He is the author of more than twenty other books on education leadership, a textbook for first year college students, several novels, and a book of essays on the music dramas of Richard Wagner. Dr. Buller has also written numerous articles on Greek and Latin literature, nineteenth- and twentieth-century opera, and college administration. From 2003 to 2005, he served as the principal English-language lecturer at the International Wagner Festival in Bayreuth, Germany. More recently, he has been active as a consultant to the Ministry of Education and many universities in Saudi Arabia, where he is helping to improve academic leadership across the kingdom. Along with Robert E. Cipriano, Dr. Buller works through ATLAS to provide leadership training and consultancy all over the world.

Other Books by Jeffrey L. Buller

- *Free Speech and Campus Civility: Promoting Challenging but Constructive Dialogue in Higher Education* (with Robert E. Cipriano)
- *Evaluating Boards and Administrators: Promoting Greater Accountability in Higher Education*
- *Confronting Today's Issues: Opportunities and Challenges for School Administrators* (with Chad Prosser and Denise Spirou)
- *A Handbook for College and University Advisory Boards* (with Dianne M. Reeves)
- *Mindful Leadership: An Insight-Based Approach to College Administration*
- *Managing Time and Stress: A Guide for Academic Leaders to Accomplish What Matters*
- *Authentic Academic Leadership: A Values-Based Approach to College Administration*
- *The Five Cultures of Academic Development: Crossing Boundaries in Higher Education Fundraising* (with Dianne M. Reeves)
- *Hire the Right Faculty Member Every Time: Best Practices in Recruiting, Selecting, and Onboarding College Professors*
- *Best Practices for Faculty Search Committees: How to Review Applications and Interview Candidates*
- *Going for the Gold: How to Become a World-Class Academic Fundraiser* (with Dianne M. Reeves)
- *World-Class Fundraising Isn't a Solo Sport: The Team Approach to Academic Fundraising* (with Dianne M. Reeves)
- *A Toolkit for College Professors* (with Robert E. Cipriano)
- *A Toolkit for Department Chairs* (with Robert E. Cipriano)

- *Building Leadership Capacity: A Guide to Best Practices* (with Walter H. Gmelch)
- *Change Leadership in Higher Education: A Practical Guide to Academic Transformation*
- *Positive Academic Leadership: How to Stop Putting Out Fires and Start Making a Difference*
- *Best Practices in Faculty Evaluation: A Practical Guide for Academic Leaders*
- *Academic Leadership Day by Day: Small Steps That Lead to Great Success*
- *The Essential Department Chair: A Comprehensive Desk Reference*, Second Edition
- *The Essential Academic Dean: A Comprehensive Desk Reference*, Second Edition
- *The Essential College Professor: A Practical Guide to an Academic Career*

More about ATLAS

ATLAS: Academic Training, Leadership, & Assessment Services offers training programs, books, and materials dealing with collegiality and positive academic leadership. Its more than fifty highly interactive programs, which can be conducted either in person or as webinars, include the following:

- Introduction to Academic Leadership
- Work-Life Balance for Academic Leaders
- Shared Governance: Only a Catchphrase?
- Time Management for Academic Leaders
- Promoting Faculty and Staff Engagement
- Best Practices in Coaching and Mentoring
- Stress Management for Academic Leaders
- Conflict Management for Academic Leaders
- Best Practices in Evaluating Administrators
- Emotional Intelligence for Academic Leaders
- Best Practices in Evaluating Faculty Members
- The Introvert's Guide to Academic Leadership
- Best Practices in Evaluating Governing Boards
- Free Speech and Campus Civility: What Works?
- Effective Communication for Academic Leaders
- Best Practices in Faculty Recruitment and Hiring
- Protecting Yourself from a Toxic Work Environment
- Best Practices in Retaining Outstanding Faculty Members
- Moving Forward: Training and Development for Advisory Boards

- The Changing Role of the Department Chair: A Longitudinal Study
- We've Got to Stop Meeting Like This: Leading Meetings Effectively
- Collegiality and Teambuilding: An Intensive Study of What Works
- Thriving in a Multi-Generational Work Environment: A Workshop for Academic Leaders
- Developing Leadership Capacity: How You Can Create a Leadership Development Program at Your Institution
- Developing Resilience as an Academic Leader: How to Bounce Back When Times Are Tough
- Why Academic Leaders Must Lead Differently: Understanding the Organizational Culture of Higher Education
- Getting Organized: Taking Control of Your Schedule, Workspace, and Habits to Get More Done in Less Time with Lower Stress
- Positive Academic Leadership: How to Stop Putting Out Fires and Start Making a Difference
- Authentic Academic Leadership: A Values-Based Approach to Academic Leadership
- Mindful Academic Leadership: A Mindfulness-Based Approach to Academic Leadership
- Fostering a College University: An In-Depth Exploration of Collegiality in Higher Education
- Managing Conflict: An In-Depth Exploration of Conflict Management in Higher Education

ATLAS offers programs in half-day, full-day, and multi-day formats. ATLAS also offers reduced prices on leadership books and sells materials that can be used to assess your institution or program:

- The Collegiality Assessment Matrix (CAM), which allows academic programs to evaluate the collegiality and civility of their faculty members in a consistent, objective, and reliable manner
- The Self-Assessment Matrix (S-AM), which is a self-evaluation version of the CAM
- The ATLAS Campus Climate and Moral Survey
- The ATLAS Faculty and Staff Engagement Survey

In addition, the ATLAS E-Newsletter addresses a variety of issues related to academic leadership and is sent free to subscribers.

For more information, contact:

ATLAS: Academic Training, Leadership, & Assessment Services
9154 Wooden Road
Raleigh, NC 27617
800-355-6742
www.atlasleadership.com
Email: questions@atlasleadership.com

www.ingramcontent.com/pod-product-compliance
Lightning Source LLC
Chambersburg PA
CBHW030144240426
43672CB00005B/266